Dedicated to
the God I serve
and my loving family
He has so graciously given me.

Lighting the Way

Again Jesus spoke to them, saying,
'I am the light of the world.
Whoever follows me will never walk in darkness
but will have the light of life.'
~ ***John 8:12***

We all have seen someone we love pass away at some point in our lives. We all grieve in different ways – some retell stories of times they spent with their loved ones, while others become quiet and withdrawn during their time of mourning. Some are relieved that their loved one is no longer suffering, while others become angry that their loved one was taken from them.

Most of us, at some point or another has been afraid of what our own death will bring. What is it like on the other side? Will anyone miss us here? What have we not yet done that we wish to do before we leave this world?

Jesus tells us that we need not fear what lies ahead, for He has brought light to the darkness of this world. Through His death and resurrection, we, too, can have eternal life. The light of Jesus' life sets an example of how we are to live and lights the way for us to everlasting life. We need not fear what lies ahead in the unknown beyond this life, for Jesus is there waiting for all who believe in Him to join Him one day. We know that our loved ones that we have lost here to this earth are waiting beside Christ for our triumphal entry into the heavenly gates when our name is called one day as well. All we have to do is follow and believe!

Prayer

Dear Jesus, thank you for lighting our way to an everlasting life with You and our Heavenly Father. Help us to not stray off of the path You have lit for us to follow. Amen.

Where Is Your Faith?

He said to them, 'Where is your faith?'
They were afraid and amazed, and said to one another,
'Who then is this, that he commands even the winds
and the water, and they obey him?'
*~ **Luke 8:25***

I am fortunate to have a church office that is located in a lovely, wooded former church camp in the middle of a built-up village near Chicago. I can still hear the sounds of traffic and sirens, yet I can still walk away from my desk to head to the coffee machine and view peaceful surroundings when my job becomes hectic. I push the button for a cup of coffee and, while it fills, I take a few more steps toward the window that overlooks the wooded grounds and sometimes small stream after a good rain and, before full foliage returns for spring and summer, a view of the edge of the adjoining cemetery. I rest my elbows on the window sill as the coffee pours into my cup, just looking out at God's creation and am reminded that everything has a season. I watch a playful squirrel jump from branch to branch or hop along the ground in search of food. A bird flits by and lands on another branch to look around and take flight once more. This is a great place to pull myself back into a peaceful mood – to regroup my mind and head back to my desk with coffee in hand to continue my tasks before me.

There are days that we sometimes wonder how we will get through what is set before us. Times that are so busy and hectic, or full of trials. What keeps us going? What keeps our feet moving ahead one step at a time during the difficult times in our lives? Faith that God has something better ahead is one thing that keeps most of us afloat during difficult times.

We may not always see the "light at the end of the tunnel," but God has promised us great things for holding tightly to our faith in Him and His Son, Jesus Christ. Sometimes our faith may seem to elude us, yet we eventually find it again.

Where is your faith during life's trials? Is it your safety line that pulls you through to better days ahead? Or have you let go and feel like you are floundering? God is still waiting to throw you a line to safety if you have let go.

Prayer

Heavenly Father, thank you for always being there to pull us through the hard times in life to the "bigger and better" future You have planned for us. Thank you for continuing to love us and care for us even when we forget that You are always beside us through "thick and thin." Please, continue to remind us that You are with us, even in the midst of our difficult times, so that we can keep holding tightly to our faith in You to keep us afloat to the future You have for us in You. Amen.

FINDING MARY IN A MARTHA WORLD

Now as they went on their way, he entered a certain village,
where a woman named Martha welcomed him into her home.
She had a sister named Mary,
who sat at the Lord's feet and listened to what he was saying.
But Martha was distracted by her many tasks;
so, she came to him and asked, 'Lord, do you not care
that my sister has left me to do all the work by myself?
Tell her then to help me.'
But the Lord answered her, 'Martha, Martha,
you are worried and distracted by many things;
there is need of only one thing.
Mary has chosen the better part,
which will not be taken away from her.'
~ Luke 10:38-42

While at the PAUMCS Conference (Professional Administrators of the United Methodist Connectional Structure) in Arizona in 2006, we had a wonderful speaker, Linda Gillis, who had been in secretarial work off and on for many years – mainly in church offices. She had written a few books about her experiences as a church secretary and at this particular conference, gave three separate talks about *"Finding Mary in a Martha World."* She even has a short story in her book, *"The Donut Theory – Meditations and Inspiration for the Church Office"* about trying to be an "M&M."

In the first session, Linda spoke about the story of Jesus arriving at the home of Martha and Mary. Martha wanted Jesus to intervene and send Mary to help her do the work of being a hostess to Jesus. Jesus reprimanded Martha in a gentle way, saying that Mary had chosen the correct decision of stopping and listening to Him. Sometimes, we feel that jobs will only be done correctly if we do them ourselves and then expect everyone else to be just as busy as we are, being jealous of the relaxed attitudes of others while we seem to do all of the work. Sometimes we over-tax ourselves when it really isn't necessary. Jesus didn't ask Martha to fix a meal or clean while He was there. What was important was to be still and listen to what He had to say.

In the second session, Linda spoke of Mary – how stopping and listening is great! We all need to take time out of our day to just sit at the feet of Jesus and listen to what He is telling us. Spend time to study His Word and meditate on what He is telling you in the verses of the Bible. How does He want us to apply what we have read in the Bible to our lives today? In the week ahead?

In the third and final session, Linda said that we really need to be a blend of Martha and Mary – be an "M&M" is her term for the combination. Yes, we need to be a "Martha" – in service – doing whatever it is that needs to be done to further God's kingdom. We also need to be a "Mary" – sitting still and listening to Jesus and His word to refresh us and lead us where He wants us to go. When we get too busy, like Martha, we tend to not stop and listen. When we sit too long listening, we don't get out and serve. Let us all strive to be a mix of "Martha" and "Mary" to be well-balanced Christians – listening and serving in this world to bring His light to those in darkness.

Prayer

Dearest Lord Jesus, we thank you for times of silent meditation at Your feet – listening to Your Word and for Your leading. We also thank you for the opportunities to share Your love to others in this world – bringing Your message of light and love to their darkened world to bring them hope and lead them to You. Continue to lead us and use us. Amen.

Don't Worry About the Tough Times

But if God so clothes the grass of the field,
which is alive today and tomorrow is thrown into the oven,
how much more will he clothe you—you of little faith!
*~ **Luke 12:28***

Looking out at the beautiful green of a spring morning, one can get lost in the newness of the season: the leaves budding overhead on the swaying branches, the daffodils, tulips and crocuses that have erupted from the ground and brighten the earth with their many colors, the grass that will soon need mowing. Going outside, we feel the warmth of the sun on our faces as the cool morning breeze blows gently across our skin. We feel spring has finally come and welcome it with excitement as all around us, things become new. God once again brings life to the earth from the dead of the former winter.

Worry begins to set back in as we take our focus off of our surroundings of spring and return to the reality of life. We still can't find a job - or if we have one, perhaps there is worry as to how long we will still be employed. We worry about paying the bills, feeding our families, how to find the proper medical care for those we love that are ill. But why do we worry so much? Do we really have that much control over our lives that we can solve all of life's many problems?

True, we do have some responsibilities in our work and how we pay for what we need, but we need to focus on God, who provides everything we need when we need it most. He will never leave or forsake us. He cares for the grass, trees, flowers - bringing them what they need to return for another springtime from the dead of winter. So, too, God will give you what you need to "stay above water" when the flood of worries try to drown you in despair. Call on God and ask for His help and guidance. He will help you, even as you go about trying to help yourself - by giving you the strength, the skills, the means by which to accomplish that which you need to accomplish. Lean on Him more often and worry less. Enjoy what He is providing you - both for your needs and for your visual enjoyment in His glorious nature around you.

Prayer

Thank you, Lord, for taking care of my every need, even when I don't realize You are helping me. Help me to always look to You for everything so that I need not worry and enjoy the life You have given me more fully. Amen.

Who Will Go?

Whom shall I send?
Who will go for us?
*~ **Isaiah 6:8***

I heard the text coming in – a cry for help from my son away at college? Yet I wasn't sure if I should jump up and answer with an "I'm coming to get you" or a "You will be fine – just hang in there" kind of answer. Deep in my mother's intuition I knew what the answer should be, yet something kept telling me to hold off – that nothing much would be gained by running to help. As the night went on, the text conversation continued back and forth, with me wanting to run and be there for my son, yet he was so far away and it was so late already. Could I even make the drive without falling asleep at the wheel? I updated immediate family of what was going on and, out of the blue, one voice jumped in and made the decision I wanted to make all along and took it upon himself to "answer the call for help" with a "you have no choice, we (your sister and her husband) are coming to get you" decision that was already made for my son in distress.

Why couldn't I answer the call and, instead, my son-in-law accompanied by my daughter jumped in to do it for me? I knew not much would be gained by running to get him, other than the comfort of being home would bring some relief to a health issue, but nothing much could be gained medically by returning home in the middle of the night. God also knew that I would fall asleep at the wheel, more than likely – I'm not as young as I used to be – like when I used to burn the candle at both ends in my younger years.

God knows who can manage His call when He needs a job done and they WILL answer "yes" to Him – although maybe not right away, like Isaiah did. Some may hesitate, like Moses, with excuses as to why they can't be the right person for the job. But, when God chooses you for a job, He will push you until you finally say "yes," because it isn't you that is doing the work alone – it is God working through you to get the job done the way He wants and when He wants it accomplished. Are you ready to answer His call?

Prayer

Dear Lord, thank you for helping us to answer Your call when You call us to do Your work in this world. Help us to continue to listen to Your voice so that we bring about Your will in this world we live in. Amen.

WE ARE FAMILY

And he replied, 'Who are my mother and my brothers?'
And looking at those who sat around him, he said,
'Here are my mother and my brothers!
Whoever does the will of God
is my brother and sister and mother.'
*~ **Mark 3:33-35***

Have you sometimes wondered why friends can sometimes seem closer than family? Family is important, don't get me wrong, but there are those special, dear friends that may seem closer to us than our blood relatives at times. Maybe there have been miscommunications within you're your blood family or you see them very little, live hundreds of miles apart from each other, or maybe the only thing you have in common is that you are related by blood. Friends, on the other hand, usually have several things in common with you that you can bond with and keep you close. One of the greatest connectional bonds is Christ!

Through Christ, we have become "adopted" into God's family – making us "brothers and sisters in Christ!" We are there for each other in good times and in bad – supporting one another through prayer – comforting one another through the difficult points in our lives and celebrating the happier moments of life together. That is what it is like in your "church family" as well as the Christian faith as a whole. We become part of a larger, loving support group than the blood family who God originally started us out with.

God has truly provided us with all that we need. Not only is He with us always, but He has given us great Christian brothers and sisters to walk together through our earthly life with so that we need never feel alone.

Prayer

Heavenly Father, thank you for giving me not only my immediate "blood-related" family, but the vast number of brothers and sisters that have been "adopted" into Your family through Christ and His saving grace. Thank you for always being with us and for giving us these siblings to walk with us through the good and bad times in our lives so that we can not only share our joy together but support each other when the burdens of life begin to weigh us down. Amen.

WHAT LIES AHEAD

For now, we see in a mirror, dimly, but then we
will see face to face. Now I know only in part;
then I will know fully, even as I have been fully known.
~ 1 Corinthians 13:12

My friend, Mary, always dreamed of going to Alaska. She hated the heat of summer and loved the coolness of winter. Mary didn't have an easy life. Years ago, her husband left her with 4 children under the age of 4 (the youngest two were twins). She came to the faith through her neighbors, and it is this faith in Christ that she hung onto strongly throughout raising her children into adulthood alone. Money was always tight, but God always managed to give her what she needed to get through whatever was facing her at the time.

When Mary was diagnosed with cancer, it was a great shock to all of us not only in her family, but in our little Bible study group that had watched our children grow from infants to Mary's oldest growing to adulthood. Mary had had no job for a couple of years, therefore, no medical insurance. She hadn't gone for annual tests that may have caught the cancer earlier, but she had no symptoms until a cough developed that wouldn't go away. Cervical cancer had spread to her lungs before showing any signs of activity in her. Chemo did not go well. She only took one treatment, which had about every bad side effect you could have. She opted for quality of life vs. quantity of life after just one treatment. She was told she would last only about 3-6 months.

Once the chemo side effects dissipated, one wouldn't have known she was sick. She had an angel help move her disability through social security and was given back pay as well. With that money, she planned her dream trip. Alaska! The last wild frontier.

She related her experiences of her trip from her hospital bed a week after she returned. (Her downhill slide in health really went quickly after her trip.) Mary said that on a whale excusion, the captain had said that on a good day, one might catch sight of one whale, or if you were really lucky, you might see a mother and her calf feeding. Mary saw TEN whales, circling a school of fish – pushing them to the middle and then the whales all rose out of the water at the same time to feed! The captain had never seen that before! Everyone was in awe. She also witnessed the glacier dropping HUGE portions of itself into the ocean – pieces as large as her double-wide trailer! Again, the captain was amazed and said that he had never seen it like that before. Mary then told those of us gathered around her bed in the hospital that, if God created this much beauty in 6 days, she couldn't wait to see what heaven was like after thousands of years!

God truly blessed Mary for her faithfulness by showing her a peek at His glorious creation and what He had in store for her. Mary lasted an amazing 11 months – much longer than the doctors had originally given her, but she is now with her Heavenly Father, to whom she remained devoted through so much adversity in her life.

If God is so good to someone with so many trials in their life and they can remain faithful and be shown God's glory and a hint of what lies ahead for remaining faithful throughout those trials, just how much more should we also remain faithful in our good times and see God's glory in those times as well, instead of taking them for granted? God is showing you daily a hint of what lies ahead. Are you looking?

Prayer

Heavenly Father, thank You for our good times and all of the wonders and beauty that You provide in our lives. We also thank You for the trials. Help us to also find Your glory throughout every experience. For everything there is a season that You alone see, and it is Your promise of Your glorious home for us that we must strive to achieve through our faith in Christ. Amen.

Do Not Despair

We are afflicted in every way, but not crushed;
perplexed, but not driven to despair;
*~ **2 Corinthians 4:8***

I have learned over the years not to say the words "things can't get any worse." It seems that if I do, something else is added to my pile of woes.

There are times in our lives when something goes wrong and we think, "things can't get any worse," only to find that, "yes, it can!" During these times, when trial after trial seems to inundate you to the brink of despair, remember that we are not alone in our trials. God is walking with us and holding us when things get to be "too much" for us to handle alone.

He will feed his flock like a shepherd;
he will gather the lambs in his arms,
and carry them in his bosom,
and gently lead the mother sheep.
*~ **Isaiah 40.11***

God will always take care of us and lead us if we will only give our troubles and worries over to Him. He will take us gently into His arms, care for and carry us through to better times ahead.

Prayer

Heavenly Father, we thank you for holding us through the difficult times in life – seeing us to better days ahead. Help us to remember to look to You instead of ourselves for the strength in difficult times and to rejoice with You when we make it through. Amen.

Slow Down

You must understand this, my beloved:
let everyone be quick to listen,
slow to speak, slow to anger;
*~ **James 1:19***

How often do you drive along and inevitably SOMEONE has the nerve to pull out on you and cause you to slam on your brakes to avoid hitting them at your current rate of speed or they go WAY below the speed limit, slowing you way down in your travel time? How quickly we feel road rage bubble up inside of us and the judgments come out about what a terrible driver that person is to do such a thing!   But do we really know what is going on with that person? Was someone or something distracting them? How often have we done the very same thing to someone else without realizing it?

I am very guilty of being judgmental of others' driving habits. I know I have made many mistakes when I have driven in the past – especially during the first few years of having my license. Yet, even though I am guilty of doing these very things, when they happen to me, I get very frustrated and judgmental of the person that has dared to get in my way.

How often do we do the same thing when someone is talking to us, or trying to tell us something? We are in a hurry and don't want to take the time to listen to what they are REALLY saying. Instead, we get frustrated with them for "getting in our way" or "slowing us down" in our own daily routine. Jesus wants us to be "quick to LISTEN, slow to speak, slow to anger." We need to learn that the world isn't here for us and our schedule, but we are here for others. A few extra minutes to really stop and listen to what someone is saying and maybe help guide them where they need to go instead of hurrying by them will make all of the difference in that person's day – that they really are important and mean something to someone instead of feeling alone or ignored. That is what Jesus wants us to do…be there for each other – showing love, compassion and mercy. Will you do what Jesus has called us to do today?

Prayer

Dear Lord, this world is such a busy, crazy place most of the time. Help us to slow down and listen to others so that we may be the love, compassion and mercy that person is looking for in their life right now. Help us to show them that they, too, are important not only to us, but to You. Amen.

ANSWERED PRAYERS

May my prayer be set before You like incense;
may the lifting up of my hands be like the evening sacrifice.
~ ***Psalm 141:2***

I have seen so many answered prayers. When asked, "Does God answer our prayers? I must respond with a very adamant and resounding "YES!" Does He always answer the way WE would like Him to answer? Again, I must respond with a resounding "NO!" God knows what is best for us and will answer accordingly. *"For surely I know the plans I have for you, says the LORD, plans for your welfare and not for harm, to give you a future with hope. ~ **Jeremiah 29.11**."*

I have seen joyful answers to prayer, as well as some with not so happy outcomes in some ways, yet God is still bringing about the welfare of those involved – not wanting to harm them, but to give them a future with hope. Harm may take on many forms, as well as healing. God's definition of "healing" may be different from ours at times. A soldier may recover physically from his wounds in battle yet be missing limbs. A child may finally be brought home after being diagnosed with something incurable yet be able to live a very normal life most of the time due to the medicines available today.

How can God use this for someone's welfare you may ask? I have also seen this in action. I have seen the wounded warrior proclaiming God's goodness and faithfulness throughout his recovery, despite having lost both legs. This same warrior, wounded just months after having married the love of his life, not only speaks to gatherings and witnesses to his faith, but his wife as well has set such a beautiful, loving example of how to love your spouse through the very toughest times and not waiver in her faith or her devotion and support to her husband – in fact, she is his biggest "cheerleader". I have seen those with incurable diseases be examples of strength and perseverance in the daily struggles of their lives and still push ahead with their faith in God fully intact – not blaming God for their situation, but instead dealing with what the Lord has set before them as a challenge to overcome and triumph over with His help through prayer and leaning on His love. I have seen instances, when people are called to prayer for others, where situations take a drastic 180° turn for the better in just a short amount of time.

God is DEFINITELY with us – answering our prayers. Don't stop praying or waiver in your faith because your desired answer to prayer is not God's answer. He knows what is best, just as a parent knows what is best for their children, and God will provide what we need when we need it. *"Pray without ceasing," ~ **1 Thessalonians 5.17**.*

Prayer

Lord, thank You for always being available to talk to and bring our deepest, heartfelt desires to. Thank You for giving us exactly what we need in answer to our requests and pleas, for You know what is best for us, even when we may think we know and are wrong. Amen.

GOD'S CREATIONS

The flowers appear on the earth;
the time of singing has come,
and the voice of the turtle-dove
is heard in our land.
~ Song of Solomon 2:12

I just love the time of year when the lilacs bloom! I love to walk up to each blooming lilac bush in my yard and just inhale its intoxicating perfume! It draws me back to my childhood, where our yard had 20 lilac bushes and the open windows would allow the gentle breeze of spring to waft the wonderful scent throughout the house. Unfortunately, this wonderful time of year only lasts a couple of short weeks before the heat of summer comes beating down on us. Yet each part of the year has its own amazing sight, sound or smell to anticipate and bring us joy.

Just as the seasons have their own respective beauty, so does each person that God has created. We often judge people by their outward appearances before even giving them a chance to show you who they really are on the inside. Each of us has been guilty of this at some time in our lives. The man that looks like a dirty "hippy" throw-back from the '70's has a heart of gold – taking in people that need a place to stay or buying an oven for a disabled lady whose oven was no longer working. The "Barbie" look-alike that one may feel is flirting with everybody else's man is really a sweet girl who is very insecure about herself and how others perceive her and has no intentions of prying someone else's man away from them – she just wants to make friends. The quiet, shy woman that is very much an introvert and doesn't stand out in a crowd has a voice like an angel and can sing like very few can. The "stuffy" business man that may, unbeknown to others, donate a large amount of money to a very worthy charity to help feed those less fortunate than himself. Each of us, made in God's image, has our own unique "beauty" that we are to share with others. You may have the beauty of a giving heart, being a very devoted friend, or sing with a voice that draws others from their chaotic state of mind into a peaceful awe of what God has created around them.

What gift or gifts has God given you to share with others? What "inner" beauty do most people not see in you until they get to know you? Use those "gifts" to be the beauty of God's creation to those that do not know Him. Draw them into a desire to find the joy that you have found in our Heavenly Father so that they, too, may bloom and grow in their season here on earth.

Prayer

Heavenly Father, what a joy you have given us in all of the differences of the seasons so that the scenery around us does not get boring. So, too, the beauty in each person you have created around us gives us reasons to celebrate Your creativity in their lives as well. Help us to show others the beauty You have created in us so that we can draw them into a life of fullness and joy in You. Amen.

BE CAREFUL HOW YOU SPEAK

Do not speak harshly to an older man,
but speak to him as to a father,
to younger men as brothers,
to older women as mothers,
to younger women as sisters
—with absolute purity.
~ 1Timothy 5:1-2

Growing up, I remember being told to always speak with respect to my elders – not that that always happened when I was upset with my parents when I didn't get my way, or with my brothers when they annoyed me. For the most part, I did speak with respect to others outside of my immediate family. Now, in public and in a former workplace I have heard foul language used as every day forms of speech (one person was speaking to or about his mother, who was also his employer) and these people feel offended if anyone calls them on it – saying that they can say what and how they want, because of freedom of speech.

A dear woman that volunteers at my church told me of a recent trip in which a man boarded the train she was on and was spouting the foulest language, which offended her and those around her. A younger woman called him out on it, to which he started spouting the foul language replies for her to mind her own business and he would speak as he wished.

What has happened to today's society? Where have respect and good manners gone? Is no one being held accountable for behaving properly in public so as not offend others? Paul wrote to Timothy that we should "not speak harshly to an older man, but speak to him as to a father, to younger men as brothers, to older women as mothers, to younger women as sisters – with absolute purity." We are to speak to one another with love and respect, not spout off foul language to upset them. *Ephesians 4.15* tells us *"But speaking the truth in love, we must grow up in every way into him who is the head, into Christ, ... "* If anything does upset you, remember to "speak in love" to those that have upset you in order to try to resolve issues. This is what Christ would call us to do as well.

Prayer

Dear Lord, help us to remember that we are all Your children and we are all adopted into one family with You as our Father. Help us to remember to always speak to each other with respect and love, no matter what issues we may not agree on or with. Help us to be more like Christ to one another in all we do and say. Amen.

Remember...

We always give thanks to God for all of you
and mention you in our prayers,
constantly remembering before our God and Father
your work of faith and labor of love
and steadfastness of hope
in our Lord Jesus Christ.
For we know, brothers and sisters beloved by God,
that he has chosen you,
because our message of the gospel came to you
not in word only, but also in power and in the Holy Spirit
and with full conviction; just as you know what kind of
people we proved to be among you for your sake.
~ 1 Thessalonians 1:2-5

Over the years, I have seen faithful Christian brothers and sisters performing selfless acts of love on behalf of the church. Some are still with us and others have gone on before us and their former "outer shell" is now lying in the cemetery just on the other side of the trees from our church. These people – both still here and gone before me – are remembered by me whenever I wander for my coffee throughout the day. I pause and look out over the small ravine and try to spy the head stones of those that have gone on before me through the leaves of the many trees between the church and their resting grounds. Their memory reminds me of those doing the work they had done before they passed, and I get a warm feeling of deep appreciation for all that they have done and for those who are now doing the work to further God's kingdom.

There are many tasks that are available to everyone within the church family – from volunteering in the office or helping with events to those that are always a welcoming smile to those just entering our church for the very first time. Some labor physically and others spiritually to do the work of the church. They seek no recognition for what they do, and they do these tasks willingly out of love for their church, church family and those less fortunate. Those of us who know who they are greatly appreciate them and remember them and their good works in our prayers and with great fondness for their devotion to their tasks. Let us all continue to remember each other in our prayers – even those who have gone on before us and have set good Christian examples for us to follow in serving Jesus Christ.

Prayer

Lord, we give You thanks and praise for those who have gone before us and set such wonderful examples of Christ's love for others for us to follow. We also give You thanks for those that continue to do Your work – especially those who seek no recognition for their many tasks done out of love for You. Help us to follow their example in serving You with loving hearts devoted to advancing Your kingdom here on earth. Amen.

Nothing and No One Is Useless

We know that all things work together for good
for those who love God,
who are called according to his purpose.
*~ **Romans 8:28***

Looking through a grove of trees, one can almost always see at least one dead tree taking up space. It is no longer producing oxygen through photosynthesis, but yet it is not wasting space, for this "dead" wood can be used for many things! It can make warm fires on cold evenings, it can be used in making pieces of art, or it can decay and become food for other "newer" plants to thrive off of.

People are the same way. No one is "useless!" We may not be able to do what we used to do, but we can still "do" things. Someone formerly active in the church that is now unable to get out anymore can write cards to others letting them know that they are supporting them through prayer or perhaps make phone calls to other shut-ins so that they have someone to talk to during an otherwise "lonely" day. Perhaps someone is retired, yet they can drive others that cannot drive to appointments or help with home repairs that others cannot do or afford themselves. A stay-at-home mom with all of her children now in school can help out another young mother with no family living nearby when that young mother needs someone to watch her children while she runs errands.

God has us all here for a purpose. We never outlive our purpose – it just may change its form of duty from time to time. What have you done to serve God in the past? Are you still able to serve in that capacity, or has your ability to serve taken a turn in a new direction?

Prayer

Heavenly Father, thank You for always allowing us a way or ways to serve You by serving others. We thank You that there is always a way to accomplish Your will, although it may take on more than one direction or job title. Help us to continue to joyfully serve You in whatever manner You will have us do so. Amen.

Blessings from Heaven

In past generations
he allowed all the nations to follow their own ways;
yet he has not left himself without a witness in doing good
giving you rains from heaven and fruitful seasons
and filling you with food and your hearts with joy.'
*~ **Acts 14:16-17***

Watching the skies turn a little darker one morning, with heavy clouds threatening rain in the distance, I was reminded that in the beautiful green of spring rain must fall. Fields begin to show signs of new growth as the first of the corn plants pop through the soil to show their little green leaves as they reach toward the sky. Trees have uncoiled their leaves from their once tiny buds into great branches of shade for shelter from the impending heat of summer.

Do I enjoy rain during the day? Only if I don't have to be out in it. I would prefer the rain fall when I am sleeping, so as to not interrupt my day by getting wet as I run from building to vehicle to building once again. This is a bit selfish on my part, for the world does not revolve around me or what I think is the best schedule of weather events. I have to live with whatever God has chosen to fill my day with and adjust accordingly.

God has always been there – knowing what is best for us. He provides food to nourish us and joy to fill our hearts. We just have to be open to His will and His ways of providing these things in our lives. We may not always like the way in which we are provided our needs, but God is there ready to give us everything we need at all times. He provides jobs to allow some people to earn a living to purchase food and find satisfaction and joy in their lives. He also provides others that are not as fortunate the ability to obtain food from food pantries. These less fortunate in the job market of today can also find joy in knowing that God loves them and is moving the hearts of others – through the joy of giving - to help make sure that they are also fed and cared for. It may not be in the way that some would like to receive from God, but God still provides for them. Sometimes we are allowed to serve others and then the tables turn, and we must allow others to serve us. We have to "swallow" our pride at times in order to receive the blessings God is giving us, but regardless, He is always there – providing for us through the generosity of others. Are we open to all the ways God is providing for us?

Prayer

Heavenly Father, we thank You for all You have given us. We may not always want to accept Your many gifts in the manner we must receive them, but help us to humble our hearts to accept all that You offer us in every way it is offered – through our own abilities that You have blessed us with as well as through the blessings of others willing to serve You by serving us in Christian love. Help us to remember that we are all Your children and one family under You, so that it is easier to accept blessings from You through each of other. Amen.

WHEN DISASTER STRIKES...

"If disaster comes upon us, the sword,
judgment, or pestilence,
or famine, we will stand before this house,
and before you, for your name is in this house,
and cry to you in our distress, and you will hear and save.
*~ **2 Chronicles 20:9***

The news reported that the people of Moore, Oklahoma had experienced a tragedy in the form of a tornado. The death toll was first reported at 51 and climbing, over 145 injured were in the hospital and over 101 were saved from the wreckage as of the next morning. Where were they to turn during such a time of tragedy? Where were they to start to help those affected? How could others be of most help to those suffering from this disaster?

In **2 Chronicles 20:9**, we are told to turn to God, for He will hear us and save. In times of so much devastation, so many injuries, so many trapped in wreckage and so much loss of life, only God is big enough to overcome all that is set before us. We need to lift everyone affected by tragedy up in prayer before God. Prayer works miracles by interceding before our mighty God for those in need. There are many other ways to help as well, but the first and most important response is prayer.

If you are one that has the ability and feel inclined to help in other ways, you can join a disaster relief team to help clear up the wreckage and rebuild communities that are devastated in the days and weeks after tragedies strike. If you have the resources, donate whatever you can to help alleviate the physical and financial losses of the victims. Yet, whatever you choose to do, continue to pray as well. God will provide the strength for those He sends to help his children in need. We must also pray that those affected will feel God's loving arms around them in the midst of their grief – giving them the strength they need to carry on in the days and weeks ahead as they rebuild their lives from such destruction and loss. How will you help others when disaster strikes?

Prayer

Lord, we cry out to You on behalf of all those affected by natural disasters. We pray for those who have lost so much in just a moment of time – homes, places of employment, loved ones that have been injured or killed in the wake of tragedy. We pray that You place Your loving arms around each and every one of them, as well as the first responders and physicians, giving them the strength and peace, they need to carry on in the days and weeks following such terrible times. Help them receive what they need from others from unaffected areas to help rebuild their lives once again and give them hope for a brighter future ahead as well as the awareness that You are with them, even in the midst of this disaster. Amen.

HOLD STEADY ON COURSE

Finally, beloved, whatever is true, whatever is honorable,
whatever is just, whatever is pure, whatever is pleasing,
whatever is commendable, if there is any excellence
and if there is anything worthy of praise,
think about these things.
Keep on doing the things that you have learned
and received and heard and seen in me,
and the God of peace will be with you.
I rejoice in the Lord greatly
that now at last you have revived your concern for me;
indeed, you were concerned for me,
but had no opportunity to show it.
Not that I am referring to being in need;
for I have learned to be content with whatever I have.
I know what it is to have little,
and I know what it is to have plenty.
In any and all circumstances
I have learned the secret of being well-fed
and of going hungry, of having plenty and of being in need.
I can do all things through him who strengthens me.
*~ **Philippians 4:8-13***

Have you ever done something and feel like you're getting nowhere or don't see any results from what you have done? Frustrating, isn't it? You feel like, "why do I even bother, anyway?"

God tells us through Paul in his letter to the Philippians to *"keep on doing the things that you have learned and received and heard and seen in me, and the God of peace will be with you."* In other words, although you may not see the results of what you are trying to accomplish in His name, He is there with you to make sure that your work is not in vain. What you do now may show results long after you are gone, so don't worry so much about how much you have accomplished in your following God's plan for you and just continue doing what He is leading you to do.

God will provide the strength for you to do whatever it is He wants you to do for Him. If you are in difficult circumstances, He is there to lead you through them. When you are going through difficult times such as bad health, financial difficulties, inability to help do certain tasks, allow God to help you with the gifts He provides in many forms as well; doctors, nurses, caregivers, financial gifts, allowing someone to complete the tasks you are unable to do at that time. If you are experiencing a time of plenty, God is there celebrating with you and wanting you to share your abundance with others less fortunate. This abundance could take many forms: wealth, good health, talents, etc. Use these gifts as He gives them to you. Whatever your situation, hold steady to the course God has set for you and hold fast to your faith in Him.

Prayer

Dear God, life can be very frustrating at times. We sometimes feel as though our work is in vain and wonder if You are even there with us. Sometimes we just want to "throw in the towel" and give up. Help us to remember that You are always there with us, through the times of plenty as well as the difficult times – giving us the strength to carry out Your will in all that we do – even if we don't see any results ourselves, for You know what the eventual outcome may be – even if it is sometime in the future that we may never see. Amen.

HIDE AND SEEK

I love those who love me,
and those who seek me diligently find me.
~ ***Proverbs 8:17***

Have you ever played a game of "Hide and Seek" when you were growing up? Part of the thrill was finding a place to hide that you felt sure you would not be found in. The other part of the game was the excitement of finding everyone that thought they could outsmart you by hiding in places they felt were impossible to be found in. Sometimes you may have succeeded in hiding somewhere that the seeker couldn't find you and you got tired of waiting in your hiding place, so you eventually came out of hiding to end the game.

Life is much like a game "Hide and Seek." We find ourselves hiding from God so that we feel safe in doing what we want to do instead of following God's will for us. Eventually, though, we "get tired of the game" and "come out of hiding" - looking for God and to "end the game."

God is never hard to find when we truly look for Him with all of our heart. He is always right beside us and knows where we are at all times, no matter how hard we try to hide from Him. He allows us to THINK we are hiding where He can't find us so that we will come to learn on our own how much we need Him and want to follow Him, but ALWAYS knows where to find us.

Prayer

Thank you, Lord, for allowing us to find within ourselves the desire to "come out of hiding" and "seek" Your will in our lives. Amen.

LOVE SUPPORT

Now we ask you, brothers and sisters,
to acknowledge those who work hard among you,
who care for you in the Lord and who admonish you.
Hold them in the highest regard in love because of their work.
Live in peace with each other. And we urge you,
brothers and sisters, warn those who are idle and disruptive,
encourage the disheartened, help the weak,
be patient with everyone. Make sure that nobody
pays back wrong for wrong, but always strive
to do what is good for each other and for everyone else.

Rejoice always, pray continually, give thanks in all
circumstances; for this is God's will for you in Christ Jesus.
~ 1 Thessalonians 5:12-18

So often it is easy for us to judge and criticize others. We think of how we could do something better or think of a better way to accomplish something. How we convey that message is not always the best way. Many of us are guilty of "chewing on shoe leather" when it comes to speaking before we think. Many times, we wish we had said or done something differently to take back the hurt we have caused inadvertently when speaking our minds.

God wants us to recognize those working hard to bring about His will in this world – even if what they are doing makes us see another side of ourselves that we would rather not see or acknowledge exists. We need to continue to love God's workers, even if we don't necessarily like or agree with the way God is using them to do His will. We also need to encourage one another in love - to speak to each other the way we would like to be spoken to. Remember the golden rule we all learned as children - "Do unto others as you would have them do unto you." We would hurt a lot fewer people's feelings if we would remember this motto from long ago and actually live by it at all times.

We are also to help others that aren't as strong as us – this is both physically and spiritually. Someone may be very strong and be able to accomplish great feats physically, but spiritually, they may be very weak and need love and support to see them through difficult times in their faith lives. I'm sure that many strong men and women have been brought to their knees during a crisis in their life, at which point they really need the strong faith and emotional support of others to get them through and show them that God is still with them.

Finally, we need to be patient with everyone. This is probably one of the hardest things for all of us. Patience is a virtue that, when anger threatens to come through the door of our emotions, is hardest to hold on to. Human nature still likes the old "eye for an eye" mentality – revenge is thought to be "sweet," yet rarely do we find total satisfaction in making others feel similar pain to ours in retaliation. We still feel that pain from the original hurt, regardless of how the other person is punished. We always feel better when doing good, so repay wrong with kindness and love. Perhaps by doing this, those doing wrong will see the joy of Christ in us and be drawn from the "dark" into the "light" of Christian life.

Prayer

Lord, we are so human and You are so divine! Our nature is so contradictory to Your will in our lives. Help us to let go of our nature of pride and make us humbly accept Your will – to show love at all times to all people. Help us not to "stir the pot," but to bring calm to the troubled waters in our midst. Help us to always rejoice in all circumstances and continually lift up all aspects of our lives to You in prayer so that we can live and be more like Christ. Amen.

DWELL ON THE POSITIVES

First, I thank my God through Jesus Christ for all of you,
because your faith is being reported all over the world. God,
whom I serve with my whole heart
in preaching the gospel of his Son,
is my witness how constantly I remember you
in my prayers at all times;
*~ **Romans 1:8-10a***

In 2012, I was fortunate enough to not only visit my nephew at Walter Reed National Medical Center in Bethesda, Maryland and see firsthand the sacrifices that some of our military men and women have made to protect our freedoms here in the United States, but also to visit the Arlington National Cemetery and see the changing of the guard at the Tomb of the Unknown. The thing I took away with me that I remember most is the attitude of these surviving military men and women who, although they have sacrificed so much, would do it all over again out of their love for this country – knowing that they had made a difference through what they had sacrificed. They also bonded with each other and gave moral support to each other during their recoveries.

Paul traveled extensively and was not always treated well when delivering the Good News throughout the countries of his time. He didn't dwell on the negatives of his ministry but delighted in the positives. He especially remembered those of new and strong faith in his prayers always. Their faith showed that he was making a difference in the world to further the message of Christ to all that he was able to during his lifetime. He longed to visit them in person and get to know them on a personal level as well instead of just from the stories of their faith that he received.

We, as Christians, are to rejoice in the faith we share and serve God wholeheartedly as well. We need to remember to hold each other up in prayer at all times as we continue to do the will of God in this crazy, mixed-up world we live in. We need to not dwell on the negatives we see but concentrate on the positives and continue pushing forward in our faith daily, knowing that we are making a difference to further the kingdom of God. Our Christian "family" is growing! Let us get to know one another better as we serve out our faith in His name.

Prayer

Heavenly Father, we remember the many sacrifices that have been made for us to be able to be called Your children. We rejoice and thank you for the many people over the centuries that have continued to carry the message of Christ throughout the world so that Your kingdom continues to grow. Use us as You will to continue the work these Christians before us faithfully passed on to us so that future generations will also come to You in faith and thanksgiving. Amen.

Going Home

Then the son said to him, "Father,
I have sinned against heaven and before you;
I am no longer worthy to be called your son."
But the father said to his slaves,
"Quickly, bring out a robe—the best one—
and put it on him;
put a ring on his finger and sandals on his feet.
And get the fatted calf and kill it,
and let us eat and celebrate;
for this son of mine was dead and is alive again;
he was lost and is found!"
And they began to celebrate.
*~ **Luke 15:21-24***

I was raised in the church – going to Sunday School and Vacation Bible School – not doubting my belief in God. However, when I was in high school, I allowed a job to take over my weekends, causing me to miss church on a weekly basis so that I could make money (minimum wage or just a few cents higher). The longer I was away from church, the easier it was to fall back on my own selfish desires. As I got a little older, I "let my hair down" and ran with my friends to places I really didn't need to be at and kept hours I shouldn't have. Burning the candle at both ends soon consumed my life – leaving little room for sleep. I totaled a car from lack of sleep, lost a love to an accident (his own, not one I was in), lost money on speeding tickets and car repairs (for the dings of not paying close enough attention to my driving). My life was not heading the direction I had always dreamed it would.

One day, I finally came to my senses. My way of life was going nowhere. I had to humble myself before God and repent of all of my selfish ways. He led me to a church where I met my husband and all of my dreams began to fall into place once I returned to God. God was always waiting for me to "come to my senses" and return "home" to Him. I just had to let go of my ways and thinking I could control my life and realize that He had everything I already wanted – and more – just waiting for me if I would only slow down and come back to Him.

Are you "running wild" and "burning the candle at both ends" trying to do all of the things you want to do? Slow down and return "home" to God. He is waiting to celebrate your return "home" so that He can satisfy all of your needs and more.

Prayer

Father in Heaven, thank You for never giving up on us as we go about our lives trying to satisfy our own needs without You. Help us all to realize that You already have everything we need and more just waiting for us. All we need to do is "come home" to You and rest in Your love and care. Amen.

Help When You Can

Do not withhold good
from those to whom it is due,
when it is in your power to do it.
Do not say to your neighbor,
'Go, and come again;
tomorrow I will give it'
—when you have it with you.
*~ **Proverbs 3:27-28***

How often do we pass by those in need? Where do we pass them by? There are so many in this world that are in need, how can we possibly help them all?

It seems just so much easier to pretend not to see them as we continue to walk on by – doing nothing to help offer them a little encouragement, hope or even a hint of their still being a human being loved by God. Yet God provides for everyone – some in different ways than others.

Times are so difficult for everyone in this economy right now. However, God doesn't say for us to help when we FEEL we have extra to give, but to give IF we have it when asked. God has put us here on this earth not to judge others, but to help each other through difficult times by sharing with each other. That also doesn't mean that others should take advantage of the generosity of others, either. This is for God to judge though, not us. We are to be His messengers of hope, love and care in this difficult world of unfairness in life. The next time you see someone in need, give them a sign of hope and love from our Heavenly Father by sharing what you have without laying judgment on those in need. God will bless you for it.

Prayer

Dear Lord, fill us and use us as your instruments of love and care for those in need to show them that they are still Your children, that You still love them and will take care of their needs. Amen.

Roadblock

I lift up my eyes to the hills—
from where will my help come?
My help comes from the LORD,
who made heaven and earth.
*~ **Psalm 121:1-2***

I work in a beautiful, wooded setting. Each season has its own beauty to admire and give me a sense of peace as I drive off of the main highway and wind my way through the trees, past the historical Boy Scout Cabin at the northwest end of the property and then continue south, up a short hill to the church parking lot. The lovely, swaying branches overhead canopy the drive in many shades of green.

One day, after the wind and rain we received the previous evening, this moment of awe was abruptly changed when, in the middle of the lane, I found that a large branch had fallen sometime during the night, blocking the continuation of my usual morning drive. It would take two or three brawny men to yank this thing off of the lane to continue on. My road was blocked! I had to back up and go up the hill on the opposite side of the property (going the wrong way in a one way), which was the only way to get up the hill that particular morning.

Occasionally in life, as we go about our daily routines, we encounter roadblocks. These could be financial issues, health issues, relational issues or even the loss of a loved one. Where do we turn to continue on? We must stop continuing on our usual course and lift our needs in prayer to God. He has created everything and controls everything. He hears us when we pray and will come to our aid. Sometimes the answers we want are not what we receive, but He does answer and help us in our time of need. Next time you encounter a "road block" in your life, stop and lift your concerns to the Lord. He will help you overcome whatever obstacle is in your way.

Prayer

Dear Lord, thank you for always hearing our cries for help and coming to our aid. Help us to always remember to turn to You first when we encounter "roadblocks" in our lives. We know You will always see us to better things ahead, even if they may not be what we want for an answer at the time. Amen.

LISTEN TO YOUR FATHER

Listen, children, to a father's instruction,
and be attentive, that you may gain insight;
for I give you good precepts:
do not forsake my teaching.
When I was a son with my father,
tender, and my mother's favorite,
he taught me, and said to me,
'Let your heart hold fast my words;
keep my commandments, and live.
*~ **Proverbs 4:1-4***

When I was growing up, I always felt I knew more than my father as far as what was best for me. I am sure I gave him a few ulcers over the years. It's amazing how, looking back... father was right! I always hated to say those words, too, because I am very competitive and hate to lose or be wrong. I failed to see that my father and mother had already gained a lot of wisdom before I was even born and they had already "seen it, done it or knew better to begin with and watched others fail in their attempts to walk through life in the wrong directions."

As I got older, moved out, got married and had my own family, I began to open my eyes and see a lot of what my father had told me was true. He had tried to see that I didn't get hurt along life's many twists and turns. Unfortunately, he could not make my final decisions; I made mistakes along the way and had to learn from them - like my overweight foot on the gas pedal, looking for a husband in the wrong places, driving offensively instead of defensively, etc.

Our Heavenly Father also tries to lead us and show us what's best for us. If only we would spend more time reading and listening to what He is telling us through His Word. We could save ourselves from so many heartaches in our lives by following His commands and directions in our lives instead of trying to make our own decisions and then earnestly pray for Him to get us out of our messes. God is the ultimate Father. He is always there to guide us, love us, care for us and - through the ultimate sacrifice of His one and only son - save us. It is when we follow what He is telling us that we truly "live" our lives to the fullest.

Prayer

Heavenly Father, we have thanked our earthly fathers for all they have done for us on their special day set aside strictly to honor them once a year. Help us to thank and honor You at all times, for, unlike earthly fathers who cannot always be with us, You are ALWAYS with us. Thank you for Your love, care and ultimate sacrifice to save us from our own mistakes in life. Amen.

The Sky's the Limit

but those who wait for the Lord
shall renew their strength,
they shall mount up with wings like eagles,
they shall run and not be weary,
they shall walk and not faint.
~ Isaiah 40:31

Orville and Wilbur Wright took four years of trial and error before they built and flew the first successful mechanical airplane. It was with much previous work with bicycles, sprockets, small motors and printing presses that they self-taught themselves engineering. It also took a lot of teamwork between these two brothers to pull off this successful creation of air transportation that most thought was impossible.

Years later, not only do we enjoy quick travel around the world because of the first air flight attempts of the Wright Brothers, but we have even put people in space and men have walked on the moon. Now we have mechanical devices exploring Mars and spacecrafts sending us pictures of planets even farther out in the universe, all from the first accomplished dreams of flight. We are still expanding our knowledge because of what two men first did in 1903. The Wright brothers would truly be amazed at what has evolved from what they first started.

You, too, can pull off what many may think is impossible when you team up with God. You can be taught by His word through Bible studies how you can follow His leading in your life. God will give you the strength you need to accomplish great feats in His name. It is amazing what you can do WITH God!

What is God leading you to do? Team up with Him now - see what you can do when God is allowed to work through you. You may even amaze yourself!

Prayer

Dear Lord, help us to look to You for strength to carry out whatever tasks You put before us to accomplish in Your name. Help us to always give You the glory for the completion of the tasks as well, for without You and Your strength, we could not do what may have seemed impossible to start with in the first place. Amen.

Not Everything Changes

remember the former things of old;
for I am God, and there is no other;
I am God, and there is no one like me,
~ Psalm 46:9

A recent trip to a town I lived in when I was a year old was fruitless when it came to finding my old home. The military town had grown to a point that I didn't know where to look for the original center of town. Mom had said we lived not far from the center of town, but I doubted I could find the home - if it even stood fifty years later. My mom couldn't remember the name of the street, but remembered details that I was looking for. Time constraints also played a role in not having enough time to look further. The building was not in the best of shape when we lived there, being a military child living off base in a southern state and military pay as it was did not allow for fancy housing. Mom remembered a fast food restaurant at one end of the street, a laundromat directly behind and a tobacco field next to our home with a barn in the back of the field.

The well-known fast food chain is still around with three locations to choose from, but I'm sure the location that my mother remembers is not one of them. After this many years, these restaurants have a habit of moving to newer buildings closer to the larger road systems that have been built. Unless I were to come back with my mom and dad, I would never be able to figure out the location on my own.

God never changes, though, and there is no one like Him. We can always find HIm, for He is everywhere at all times. We remember the stories from the Bible that we grew up with that showed His faithfulness to His people. His faithfulness continues today. He is still here, but now for all who believe in His Son's saving grace. In a world where things are constantly changing, it is wonderful to know that we will always have a constant, unchanging God that will always be there to love us, guide us and save us. We have only to look for Him and He is there.

Prayer

God in Heaven, what a comfort it is to know that, when everything else is changing around us, You will never change. You are always there for us - loving us through everything. Thank you for Your constant companionship. Help us to always look for You during our day-to-day activities and realize that You will never leave us. Amen.

Trying New Things May Amaze You

'Salt is good; but if salt has lost its taste,
how can its saltiness be restored?
*~ **Luke 14:34***

I had never tried the southern dish chicken and waffles until later in life. I had always thought it was a crazy idea and would never have put the two items together on my plate, but they came highly recommended by our concierge at the hotel desk when she recommended a restaurant around the corner and down the street a couple of blocks from the hotel. I thought that I would be brave and try her recommendation. Oh my goodness! I was blown away! What had I been missing all of these years? A combination of sweet and salty - crunchy and soft - juicy and buttery - all rolled into one plate of amazing flavors!

Our Christian faith is much like this dish. We often try to adjust our faith to fit our comfort level in our lives. Some of us choose to quietly study the Bible on our own, while others choose to join groups to learn more about their faith with the help of others. Some choose to donate items for those in need, while others choose to "get out in the field" and do actual mission work. When we choose not to put our faith into action - only believing, but not showing any of our faith to others, we are like salt that has lost its saltiness. Once salt loses its saltiness, it isn't worth anything and must be thrown out.

Unlike salt, though, our faith can be re-energized and restored. We can choose to become more involved in sharing our faith with others and learning more about Christ through

Bible studies. Expanding our faith life is like expanding our decisions about trying new dishes and food combinations. We just have to make that decision for ourselves to try to share our faith in new ways and we may blow our minds with how amazingly our choices in sharing our faith not only transforms us, but transforms others around us.

Prayer

Dear Lord, the wonderful Christian life that You have provided for us to share has so many facets to expand on and share with others around us. Help us to step out of our comfort zone and experiment with new ways to share our faith with others . May we not only grow through this sharing, but bring others to this same exciting faith journey as well. Amen.

GAINING WISDOM AND UNDERSTANDING

'God understands the way to it,
and he knows its place.
For he looks to the ends of the earth,
and sees everything under the heavens.
When he gave to the wind its weight,
and apportioned out the waters by measure;
when he made a decree for the rain,
and a way for the thunderbolt;
then he saw it and declared it;
he established it, and searched it out.
And he said to humankind,
"Truly, the fear of the Lord, that is wisdom;
and to depart from evil is understanding." '
*~ **Job 28:23-28***

Driving along the Florida Keys, You see a lot of scrubby looking foliage - not really attractive to the eye and too tall to allow you to see what lies beyond. After driving for miles, there are breaks in the scenery, when the waters come nearer the road or you cross a bridge to the next island. The amazing colors of the waters that you see no where else in the continental U.S. - turning to different shades of aqua, sea foam green and deep blues - sometimes all at once in patches defined by the differing depths of the waters. At first thought, you might think, "Why don't they just tear all of that ugly growth out and landscape it to look more beautiful and allow you to see more of the water and land that lie behind it?"

God has more wisdom than the human mind, though. The Keys have been subject to hurricanes and tropical storms through the centuries and these unattractive plants are what

56

help hold this series of islands in place. These plants are able to survive in the combination of salty and non-salt waters. To get rid of them would, in essence, cause the islands to wash away in the storms.

When difficult circumstances come into our lives, God does not celebrate our trials, but He does have all wisdom and knowledge to see us through and make us stronger. To walk away from God in difficult times will only lead to more hardships in life. Staying true to God - even through the storms of life - leads to a deeper understanding of His love and faithfulness to those who trust in Him. Hold on to God tightly in all circumstances, just as the roots of the tropical plants hold the sands of the islands in place.

Prayer

Heavenly Father, You have made such wonders and beauty all around us. Help us to appreciate even the things that may not be beautiful to us, for You have a reason for everything You have placed here on this earth. Help us to also hold fast to You - during the good and the bad times of life. Help us to always remember that You have a reason for everything that we must go through in life and that by holding on to You, we will get through anything and gain understanding and wisdom. Amen.

WITHERING BEAUTY

For All flesh is like grass
and all its glory like the flower of grass.
The grass withers,
and the flower falls,
but the word of the Lord endures for ever.'
That word is the good news that was announced to you.
~ 1 Peter 1:24-25

The beauty of the surroundings, no matter where you are, are fleeting. Years cause decay of beautiful architecture and plants wither and die off. New plants take their place. New buildings are built where old ones have rotted away and been torn down. People are born, live, die and are forgotten, aside from a few that have left legacies that seem to transcend the rule of "dust to dust." What some have done in their lives seems to keep their memories alive longer than most. But even what they have created will eventually turn to dust. Nothing is forever, so it seems…or is it?

The Word of our Heavenly Father is eternal. It has not changed and has been handed down from generation to generation. The history of mankind and their relationships with God are told in one, holy book - the Bible! Just like our Lord, His Word has always been here and will remain long after we are gone. Studying His Word, meditating on it and applying it to our lives helps us to continue passing this great treasure down to later generations to come. It is a true story of love and faithfulness that all are welcome to be a part of and will never wither away.

Prayer

Eternal Father, what a treasure Your Word is to us! What a guiding light it is in this dark world we live in. Help us to study Your Word - gleaning from it what You wish us to learn and apply in our lives to continue handing this wonderful gift to all those around us now and in the future. Amen.

GOD ANSWERS YOUR CALL

When they call to me, I will answer them;
I will be with them in trouble,
I will rescue them and honor them.
~ Psalm 91:15

My husband and I began our married life always including prayers at mealtime. We still pray a similar prayer each day, including requests for healing, guidance and to be kept safe throughout the coming week. My husband and son were on a mini father-son excursion to Amish territory in my husband's new car. He drives safely – rarely going over the speed limit and is very defensive in nature when he sees something that may cause a collision. He uses proper signaling and allows sufficient spacing so as not to create a hazard to others when turning. Despite doing everything that he should to keep from causing an accident, the semi driver behind him must not have been paying close enough attention to his own driving. While waiting to turn left at a green light and waiting for oncoming traffic to clear, the semi driver saw the car ahead of my husband complete his left turn and either assumed my husband would follow immediately behind the first car, or was distracted by something else. Either way, he proceeded to pull forward into his turn while my husband remained in a stopped position and rear-ended the car. My husband and son were not injured, but my husband kept wondering, "Why me? I did everything I was supposed to. Why did I have to be hit?"

God was watching out for my family, as we request daily in our prayers. They were safe from harm, despite the damage to the car (and the truck driver's ego). God saw the trouble my family was in, even though they didn't see it themselves, and saved them from injury. God answered our often prayed request for "safety throughout the coming week," even when the danger wasn't seen coming.

God is watching out for all who call on His name. He will remain with you in troubles you are aware of as well as those that you do not foresee coming upon you. He will rescue you and honor you. All you have to do is ask. Are you calling out to God? He is there and He is answering your call.

Prayer

Lord, thank you for Your constant vigil over us – for answering our call for Your healing, guidance and safety, even when we don't see something bad coming our way. Thank You for Saving us and honoring our calls for Your help in our lives. Amen.

Help in Any Way You Can

I commend to you our sister Phoebe,
a deacon of the church at Cenchreae,
so that you may welcome her in the Lord
as is fitting for the saints,
and help her in whatever she may require from you,
for she has been a benefactor of many and of myself as well.
*~ **Romans 16:1-2***

Paul was writing to the church in Rome, asking them to take care of Phoebe – to welcome her and help her with whatever she needed them to do, for she had aided many, including Paul, in his ministry. It always helps add credibility to someone when they are given a "letter of recommendation" by someone that is viewed as "in a high position of authority." Paul, who had been in contact with the Roman church, knew that the congregation would be more willing to help Phoebe if he gave a recommendation of her to them. They were to help in any way they could to carry on whatever she was led to do to further God's kingdom.

We, too, have many opportunities within our church, in the local area, and elsewhere to help "in any way we can" to further God's kingdom. We can do mission work through our church, work at food pantries or soup kitchens, join a mission team, or donate to victims of weather tragedies. We can even help with special events within our church to help raise funds for the operating expenses of the church itself to ensure that it can meet the needs of its own church family as well as those who are seeking a closer connection to God – either returning to the faith they have been away from for awhile or coming to the faith for the first time in their life.

The third Saturday of September, our church holds their Annual Campground Festival. Not only is it a time to help raise funds for the church, but it is also a time to connect with other members of the church and get to know them better by working with them toward a common goal. This day is full of opportunities for work, fun and fellowship.

If you haven't already committed to helping out your church family, it's not too late! There is always something for you to do when you are willing to help in any way you can - be it a special event, a mission opportunity or visiting those who are no longer able to get to church. There is a satisfaction in doing the work God is calling you to do.

Prayer

Dear Heavenly Father, help us to look within ourselves and find the energy and willingness to help further Your kingdom in any way we can. Amen.

LET US GATHER TOGETHER

For where two or three
are gathered in my name,
I am there among them.'
~ ***Matthew 18:20***

Throughout history, there have been festivals and annual celebrations that the Jewish people have kept to remember their heritage and to thank God for all He has given them. There are also times to gather to remember and mourn, as did the disciples after Jesus' crucifixion. In each instance, God has always been there among them – celebrating and mourning with them.

We still gather for many reasons today. There are religious holidays, birthdays, weddings, births, deaths and funerals. We still celebrate festivals for various reasons. We, as Christians, gather to worship God together as one family of faith. We meet for special Healing Services to anoint those suffering physical, emotional or spiritual pain in their lives and pray for their restoration to a healthy, God-filled life of peace. We hold special alternative contemporary worship services in hopes of drawing the un-churched into the faith in a way that is more comfortable for them to worship in and draw closer to God. No matter what the reason, God is still with us every time we gather, just as He has been for His people since the beginning of time.

When our church holds special events, God will be with us as we gather together to work, fellowship, enjoy making new friends within our church family and those new among us. These are times that we can share our faith with each other while God is right beside us, as always. We can demonstrate His love for others through our service to Him on days like this. These events, although meant to help raise funds for our church's operating expenses, really are more than that. These are opportunities to bring others to faith in Christ and to deepen our own faith as well as deepening the faith of others around us. Everyone needs to enjoy these events and look for the many ways God touches our lives through them.

Prayer

Dear God, thank You for the many gatherings we attend throughout our lives. These are times to feel closer to each other and to You. Thank you for the many opportunities that these gatherings allow for us to grow in our faith and in relationship with You and other Christians around us, as well as to draw others to You in faith. Amen.

"Ahhhh" Moments

God saw everything that he had made,
and indeed, it was very good.
And there was evening
and there was morning, the sixth day.
*~ **Genesis 1:31***

Do you remember the song by Mac Davis, ***"Stop and Smell the Roses?"*** The refrain *"You're gonna find your way to heaven is a rough and rocky road, if you don't stop and smell the roses along the way,"* came to mind one morning as I stepped out of the house and locked my door. Not five yards from me were two beautiful fawns, which of course, I startled. They immediately sprinted to the back of my yard and found that they had their escape blocked by a fence and my shed.

I paused and spoke softly to them to not to be afraid and that I wasn't going to hurt them as I walked away from them toward my van to leave for work. They stopped and watched me not try to approach them further. One boldly moved closer to the house, yet still away from me and "hid" in the shadow of my lilac bushes. The other soon joined him and they both watched me get into my van and pull away – as I was not trying to harm them. I hope they realize that my back yard is a safe haven for them. This is not the first time I have seen deer in my yard – even though I live on the edge of a suburban town near a busy road. I have seen a mother deer laying under my oak tree with her fawn a year or so ago. I have even seen a doe walk down the middle of my street in late afternoon.

God has created amazing beauty all around us, but our busy lives often cause us to miss this beauty as we hurry from one place to another. We need to slow down and look at all of the wonders God has placed before us for our enjoyment. The beauty of the seasons and nature itself are here for us to take in and just meditate on how wonderful God is to have provided all of this for us. Even God stepped back after He created everything and saw that it was "very good." If God can take the time out of His schedule to just step back and say "Ahhh, this is good," shouldn't we also take that same time to appreciate all of creation around us? Look for an "Ahhh" moment today and thank God for that special time in your day.

Prayer

Dear Heavenly Father, thank You for all You have made for us and provided for us in our lives. Help us to take the time to appreciate Your beautiful creations around us and to say "thank You" when we see them. Amen.

Stay Awake

Then he came to the disciples
and found them sleeping; and he said to Peter,
'So, could you not stay awake with me one hour?
*~ **Matthew 26:40***

Riding along in the car, especially during what I consider "boring" scenery or too familiar of an area, I often allow the hum of the tires lull me to sleep, much to the dismay of my husband. All too often, I will feel a nudge of my arm and hear a "you're sleeping again" from him as he continues the drive to wherever we are heading. Sometimes, trying as hard as I might to fight to keep my eyes open, even during some good scenery, I still find myself falling asleep.

Christ's disciples also found it difficult to stay awake while Jesus walked farther on to pray. He came back several times to only find them once again asleep. Their vigilance was lacking.

What He is really wanting from all of us in this verse, though, is to stay alert to what is around us. We are not to allow evil to come to steal us from Him. We must be ready for when He returns, for it will be at a time that only God knows and could be just around the corner.

Prayer

Dear Lord, help us all to "stay awake" - alert for Your return.
Come soon, Lord. We are ready for Your kingdom to come.
Amen.

Don't Take the Shortcuts

But his master replied, "You wicked and lazy slave!
You knew, did you, that I reap where I did not sow,
and gather where I did not scatter?
Then you ought to have invested my money with the bankers,
and on my return I would have received what was my own
with interest. So take the talent from him, and give it
to the one with the ten talents. For to all those who have,
more will be given, and they will have an abundance;
but from those who have nothing,
even what they have will be taken away.
~ Matthew 25:26-29

On an early fall morning as I looked out my window, I noticed a fine cobweb running across the outside of the glass. Just above this, there were a couple of small feathers and below that, a bird "deposit" from hitting the glass. At night, the lights within the building attract insects that head toward it. These insects soon find that they are "caught up" in the invisible snare awaiting them across the glass that the light is attracting them through. The bird, perhaps thinking that the window was open and it had a "shortcut" to the other side of the building soon found that it had "knocked itself silly" by running into the clear glass blocking its journey abruptly.

People often look for shortcuts in life. High stakes gambling or lotteries are sometimes thought to be the "ticket" needed to better their financial lot in life. Hanging around influential people that might not be very reputable might accelerate their ascent in the workplace or society. What are the costs of these so called "shortcuts"? Loss of money? Loss of reputation or family and friends? Are shortcuts really all they are cracked up to be?

Most people that gamble and play the lottery are the ones least likely to have the money to spare on such a folly to improve their finances. In the end, most end up worse off than when they began. Some lose everything – home, work, family and friends – trying to win it big!

Those that use other people for the purpose of advancement also often come out losers. They may neglect those that really care for them while spending time with those they think can move them up at work or in society. Sometimes this includes losing one's reputation, family and friends to earn this "bump up" in their lives. Getting to the top may not be as wonderful as anticipated if people don't have the ones they love there to share it with them. It only becomes a hollow victory.

God does not intend for everyone to "have it all" in the way of money and position. God's values are not always the same as ours. God provides us with the talents and all that we need to further His kingdom here on earth, not for us to exploit for our own gain. God has a unique plan for each of us and a path on which we must travel to serve out His plan. It might not be the "shortcut to money and fame", but it will end with a reward for our dedication in using His gifts according to His plan and purpose in our lives. Our reward is certain. The timing is God's, not our own. It may or may not be on this earth in this lifetime, but rather in the eternal life to come. Don't take the shortcuts. They aren't always as wonderful as they appear.

Prayer

Dear Lord, thank you for all you have given us. Help us to appreciate what we have and to use it for Your glory and not our own. Any surplus You provide is not ours alone, but to be shared to further Your kingdom here on earth. Keep us from trying shortcuts to further our own lot in life. Help us to be patient and allow Your plan to unfold in our lives. In the name of Your precious son Jesus Christ. Amen.

CELEBRATE

'Return to your home,
and declare how much God has done for you.'
So he went away, proclaiming throughout the city
how much Jesus had done for him.
~ Luke 8:39

My nephew, who was injured in Afghanistan, was greeted by his community in a "Welcome Home" celebration. There was be a parade, a speech, bands, raffles, drawings, kiddie activities, t-shirts – you name it. It was one great big gathering to say "thank you" to all that have supported him in his recovery as well as for the community to thank him for his service and sacrifice for his country.

We are to also *"declare how much God has done"* for us! We need to go out and celebrate the wonderful works of our Heavenly Father in our lives – thanking Him as well as showing others how great and marvelous He is. We need to constantly thank and praise our God for our lives and all He has provided for us – the home we have, the food we eat, the love of friends and family around us, our health and for physicians that work to restore our health to us when we are not well. We need to draw together as a community of faith – as in the old days of the old camp meetings – to renew our covenant with God to remain faithful to Him, to spread the good news of His saving grace to others, and live our lives as He wishes us to live them.

Let the celebration begin!

Prayer

Heavenly Father, thank You for all of Your marvelous gifts You have provided us in our lives. Let us constantly be in a state of celebration in our lives by proclaiming Your love and grace to others. Amen. 72

WELL DONE!

*His master said to him, "Well done, good
and trustworthy servant; you have been trustworthy
in a few things, I will put you in charge of many things;
enter into the joy of your master."*
~ *Matthew 25:21*

One weekend, our church family held a celebration honoring a beautiful woman of Christ. Her 34 years of ministry through directing the children's choirs with her love and grace have touched the lives of many over the years – some of the children she has directed now have or have also had children of their own directed by her as well. We had a special presentation honoring her during our worship services on a Sunday as she retired from this position she had held near and dear to her heart all of these years, complete with posters and pictures taken throughout her years of service, with her church family telling her just how much we have appreciated her faithful ministry.

Christ trusts us to carry out His ministry in this world. He puts us in charge of different tasks according to our different abilities and expects us to fulfill those that He has set before us. As we go about these tasks we are entrusted with, we find great joy and fulfillment in our lives. Someday, we will be called upon by Him to answer for what we have accomplished in our lives. At that time, we also hope to hear the words "Well done, good and trustworthy servant!"

How is your "task" list coming along?

Prayer

Dearest Lord Jesus, thank You for setting before us tasks that, with Your help, we can accomplish. Help us to fulfill them according to Your will so that one day we will hear You say, "Well done, good and trustworthy servant!" Amen.

LET THE CELEBRATION BEGIN!

They shall celebrate the fame
of your abundant goodness,
and shall sing aloud
of your righteousness.
~ Psalm 145:7

The 4th of July did not become a federal holiday until 1941. This day of remembering and celebrating our patriotism is marked by parades, fireworks, picnics, carnivals, etc. We always look forward to holidays like these to take a day off of work and just have fun and enjoy the company of friends and family. Patriotic songs proclaim the goodness of God in seeing us through to our freedom as a new nation. When the 4th of July falling in the middle of the week, many communities will continue this annual celebration throughout the following weekend.

We, as Christians, need to remember that every day is a day to celebrate the goodness and grace of God. He continually provides for our every need, therefore, there is not really one "set" day to celebrate His greatness. Yes, we tend to set aside one day a week to gather with our church family to worship Him, but every day is a good day to celebrate God's loving kindness to us and others. When we wake up in the morning, we can celebrate in a prayer of thanksgiving for yet another day to live according to His will. When we go about our business throughout the day, we can lift up praises for the many opportunities and gifts He provides for us. When we lay our heads down at night, we can again thank Him for blessing us throughout our day. Every day has something to be thankful for and to celebrate.

What do you see in your life today to celebrate with God?

Prayer

Lord, thank you for yet another beautiful day to live our lives according to Your will. Help us to lift praises up to You throughout the day, allowing You to celebrate with us the lives You have given us to live. Let our celebratory lives lift others' hearts to celebrate with You all the days of their lives as well. Amen.

CHILD-LIKE FAITH

but Jesus said,
'Let the little children come to me,
and do not stop them;
for it is to such as these
that the kingdom of heaven belongs.'
*~ **Matthew 19:14***

Vacation Bible School began with many youngsters eagerly joining in the lessons, games, songs and fellowship of "Kingdom Rock!" What a joy it was to see the children throughout the church building learning about Christ and His love for them and all those around them. Children are like sponges – they absorb all of this information and carry it home to share with others in their family and their friends in the neighborhood. The songs they learn may be heard during the car rides home and throughout their homes as they go about the remainder of their day with the music still playing through their heads. They may chatter up a storm at the dinner table as they relate all that they experienced at VBS.

If only we adults had the same eagerness to learn about our Lord and Savior! That would be amazing! To pull out our Bible and read a little bit each day to better acquaint ourselves once again to the Jesus we knew as children or even to just get to know Him for the first time in our lives would be such a gift to our Heavenly Father. Christ would be smiling to see us singing the old, familiar hymns or the newer contemporary songs of praise throughout our daily tasks or as we travel from place to place doing our errands. Best of all would be for us to be like little children – excitedly sharing this faith of ours with all those around us.

Are you ready to become like a child again? Jump into your Bible, turn on the Christian radio stations and start living the joyful life of a child of God!

Prayer

Lord, sometimes we would love to "turn back the clock" and become children again. Help us to find our child-like faith in You and share it with others, for when our hearts are full of faith in You, we are once again "young at heart" as we eagerly await Your kingdom. Amen.

CANDLELIGHT

You shall put these words of mine
in your heart and soul, and you shall bind them
as a sign on your hand,
and fix them as an emblem on your forehead
*~ **Deuteronomy 11:18***

I saw a group of children making candles the old-fashioned way – by continually dipping a cord into melted wax, allowing it to set and re-dipping until the candle reaches the desired thickness. The children were excited to be doing a "messy" craft – done outside, of course, so the melted wax that dripped off of the candles would fall onto the asphalt instead of the carpeting inside. The candles were then "draped" over a line to finish setting up while the children went about other activities.

Like the wax of the candle on a cord, we can "coat" our heart with the Word of God. As we study the Bible each day, we allow a layer of knowledge from His Holy Word to "set up" on our heart. We can meditate and dwell on what we read each day, allowing that "layer" of knowledge to set into our hearts before adding another layer the next day. Our hearts become a "candle" for God's love and can "light the way" for others to find their faith in God as we allow His light to "shine" through all we do.

Prayer

Heavenly Father, help us to make the time to "coat" our hearts and minds with Your Word, so that we can let our light shine for all to see. Amen.

Only One Per Day

Finally, brothers and sisters,
we ask and urge you in the Lord Jesus that,
as you learned from us how you ought to live
and to please God (as, in fact, you are doing),
you should do so more and more.
~ 1 Thessalonians 4:1

On my desk I have a little sign that reads, "I can only please one person per day...Today is not your day. Tomorrow is not looking good either." I have to chuckle at that sign, because I really don't abide by that credo. Or do I? If I change the word "person" to "entity," perhaps I am living by that motto.

If I live to please only one "entity," that would be to please God. By pleasing God, I am doing what God asks of me – to live more and more like Christ. True, I am not out to "please" others by giving them everything they want, but I am here to serve others in the name of the Lord. I give of my time, talents and Christian love.

Therefore, it looks as though I may be living by the little credo on my desk after all. By putting God first, I may also please others through the service I do in His name. There is always more I can do to please Him each day. I just have to look to Christ for my example to follow.

Prayer

Heavenly Father, may I always put Your wishes before my own so that my life may be a pleasing sacrifice to You. Amen.

KINGDOM OF EXCITEMENT AND JOY

He said therefore,
'What is the kingdom of God like?
And to what should I compare it?
It is like a mustard seed
that someone took and sowed in the garden;
it grew and became a tree,
and the birds of the air made nests in its branches.'
~ Luke 13:18-19

"Kingdom Rock" had just wrapped up at our church's Vacation Bible School. The excitement the children entered the building with each day was such a joy to see. One mother even told me that her youngest child couldn't wait to get here, exclaiming as soon as he got up in the morning, "Are we leaving for Holy Bible School yet?" Some children hated to have the week of fun and learning about Jesus end. But does it really end here?

The children got a taste of God's love in a medieval kingdom theme. God's Word also describes heaven as the *"kingdom of God."* Questions have been raised for centuries asking what heaven is like.

Jesus often replied to this question in parables, one of which compares heaven to a planted mustard seed. If we look at this parable closer, we can see that something that seems so very small is really much larger when it comes to its ultimate completion and many find rest and comfort in its branches. If we look at it in this way, heaven seems so small and far away, yet, someday, we will see it in all of its enormity and splendor and also find comfort and rest in this final destination. Heaven is the ultimate goal for which we strive to achieve an eternity of peace, and the excitement in which we will one day enter it will be far more than we can ever imagine.

Prayer

Almighty God, we thank You for these wonderful opportunities to teach Your children about You and Your Kingdom. May we all be able to experience the ultimate joy and excitement of entering Your kingdom one day with even more enthusiasm than we can ever imagine possible. Amen.

Confusion Made Clear

For we know that the law is spiritual;
but I am of the flesh, sold into slavery under sin.
I do not understand my own actions.
For I do not do what I want, but I do the very thing I hate.
Now if I do what I do not want, I agree that the law is good.
But in fact it is no longer I that do it, but sin that dwells
within me. For I know that nothing good dwells within me,
that is, in my flesh. I can will what is right, but I cannot do it.
For I do not do the good I want, but the evil I do not want
is what I do.Now if I do what I do not want, it is no longer I
that do it, but sin that dwells within me.
*~ **Romans 7:14-20***

Years ago, four other ladies and I would meet weekly to study the Bible while our children played together. The above verses became an "inside joke" to us when we would come upon passages that were difficult for us to comprehend at first. We learned that to understand these verses (written in Paul's "legal-speak" language), we really needed to break them down and go over them slowly. Once we took the verses apart and studied them a little at a time, the meaning became clearer. Other passages needed to be tackled in the same manner, but this one was always the hardest to understand when being read aloud at a normal pace. As soon as we would come upon a difficult passage, one of us would start to say, " we do what we don't want to do, not what we want to do…" and begin to chuckle. Then we would "get down to business" and start breaking down the difficult passage to better understand what God was trying to say to us.

These verses explain how we were born into a sinful world, to which our sinful nature comes naturally to us. The law is from God, therefore, it is spiritual – not of this world and more difficult for us to follow. As Christians, we sometimes battle our sinful nature from within, because our sinful nature comes so much easier to us than to follow the spiritual law of God. We want to follow the law, but at times our sinful nature has a habit of "popping up," causing us to do the very things we know we shouldn't do. To follow God's law requires concentration and determination to overcome our natural instincts of sin to which we were born, even when we know that to follow God's law is the good and right thing to do.

This is a battle we live with as Christians every day. In order to live according to the law of God, we need to arm ourselves for doing battle against our natural instincts of the sinful nature that we were born with. We can win the battle of confusing decision making with the clarity of God's direction given to us through daily prayerful communication with Him and by studying the Bible to discover His battle plan given to us centuries ago. We can arm ourselves against our sinful natures so that we will have the strength and knowledge to fight the easier ways of our sinful nature from overtaking our desire to follow God with our whole heart. Every day is a day to ready ourselves for battle. Get your armor of God on and set out to fight the good fight!

Prayer

Lord God, this fight between doing the right thing vs. wrong thing in life is a constant battle of wills between the evil nature we were born into and the knowledge of the good we have accepted into our lives through the saving grace of Your Son, Jesus Christ. Help us to arm ourselves with Your strength and knowledge to go against the evil around us so that we can fight the good fight to bring others to You through our example on how to live in this world so that we can one day join You in Your kingdom. Amen.

Welcoming a Stranger

Then the righteous will answer him,
"Lord, when was it that we saw you hungry
and gave you food, or thirsty
and gave you something to drink?
And when was it that we saw you a stranger
and welcomed you, or naked and gave you clothing?
And when was it that we saw you sick
or in prison and visited you?"
And the king will answer them,
"Truly I tell you, just as you did it to one of the least of these
who are members of my family, you did it to me."
*~ **Matthew 25:37-40***

Our church had a collection of items and funds to help set up a family who had been persecuted in another country. They had come to America to start all over again in a safe environment – bringing nothing of their own. This was a larger family than we first expected – thinking it would be a family of about four, we later found out it was a family of nine! The giving increased by our church family to make a home for this new family that was starting out with nothing to make a new life here among our neighbors. They are not of any religious background or ethnicity that we share in our church, however, we were called by Christ to help the stranger. What better way to bring the love of Christ to others than to set them up for success in a new country with a better chance at a new life? What better way to show them that our faith and beliefs are not a danger to their way of living? What better way to show them that we can live in peace with one another as opposed to what they experienced in their own country?

Christ said that we were to fill the needs of those around us, for by doing so, we were serving Him. He didn't say to only serve those that believed as we do, nor did He say only to show mercy to those that are like us. He said, *"just as you did it to one of the least of these who are members of my family, you did it to me."*

Who are Christ's family? All those that believe that He is the promised Messiah that died and rose again to pay for all that we have done wrong in our lives. One might ask how someone of another faith can be a member of Christ's family if they don't believe as we do. Although they do not currently share our faith, they may come to know Christ through the love that we share with them, so even if they are not currently be members of Christ's family, they may come to believe in Him as their Savior by caring for and serving them as if we were serving Christ. Our serving them may touch upon their lives in a way that opens their hearts to hearing about and accepting Christ as their savior, so that by the time we answer for what we have done in our lives in Christ's name one day, these strangers may also be members of Christ's family with us.

Prayer

Heavenly Father, help us to open our hearts and minds to serve not only those that already believe in Your Son as their personal Savior, but also those that do not know You or Your Son, so that, through our loving service, they may come to know and accept You into their lives and become a member of Your family with us. Amen.

Seeing Clearly

Or how can you say to your neighbor,
"Friend, let me take out the speck in your eye",
when you yourself do not see the log in your own eye?
You hypocrite, first take the log out of your own eye,
and then you will see clearly
to take the speck out of your neighbor's eye.
~ Luke 6:42

Have you ever had something irritating your eye so badly that, not only could you hardly keep the irritated eye open, the good eye also wanted to remain shut? It is very difficult to see clearly with your eyes battling to stay open as they burn and tear up from whatever foreign object or injury is obscuring your view. Yes, you can see, but with much strain and difficulty focusing on what you are actually viewing, due to the discomfort you are trying to ignore while trying to see where you are going or what is just up ahead of you.

The same can be true in trying to solve others' problems. If we have difficulties clouding our lives and distracting us from being able to clearly see resolutions to our own problems, it makes it difficult for us to concentrate and truly see someone else's problems and give them clear direction in how they should be living their lives. It might make us temporarily feel better to ignore our own discomfort and problems by pointing out someone else's and trying to give them advice as to how they should be living, but it would serve others better to first take care of our own issues before trying to tell someone how to fix theirs.

No one can give better solutions to our troubles than Christ, for He was the only one that had no issues of His own to cloud

His views of situations. Others had trouble with Christ and how He was telling them they should be living, but Christ had no vices with which He needed to be rid of, or sins that He needed to try to hide from others around Him. He is the only source of perfect advice on how to live and what we should strive for in life. If anyone is having a problem in their lives, they need only turn to Christ for direction and solutions to their difficult circumstances. He will give them what they need to turn their lives in the right direction and go forward – seeing clearly where they need to go in life to live according to God's will.

Prayer

Dear Lord, help us to stop trying to make ourselves feel better about ourselves by pointing out others' faults and instead look to You to solve our own problems in how we are living our lives. Help us to clearly see where You want us to go to serve You with the lives You have given us, so that perhaps, others can follow our example and look to You as well. Amen.

The Thirst Quencher

Jacob's well was there, and Jesus,
tired out by his journey, was sitting by the well.
It was about noon. A Samaritan woman came to draw water,
and Jesus said to her, 'Give me a drink.'

Jesus said to her, '
Everyone who drinks of this water will be thirsty again,
but those who drink of the water that I will give them
will never be thirsty. The water that I will give
will become in them a spring of water
gushing up to eternal life.'
*~ **John 4:6-7, 13-14***

On one of our hottest summer days, the heat index was well over 100° F. To try to stay hydrated in this type of heat seemed almost impossible if we had to be out in it for any length of time. Going in and out of the air-conditioning also taxed the body - making us feel tired and in need of a good, long nap!

Jesus didn't have the luxury of an air-conditioned vehicle to travel in. He walked everywhere. As He traveled, He tired and became thirsty just like everyone else, although we often find it difficult to believe. Jesus was fully human and fully divine all at the same time. When He asked the Samaritan woman for a drink, anyone of the Jewish faith would have been shocked to see Jesus even talking to this woman, since in the Jewish culture, associating with a Samaritan was like associating with a dog – considered well beneath their stature in life. Jesus also offered her "spiritual water" – that will become like a spring welling up inside her so that she would never thirst again and will give her eternal life. This "spiritual water" is for all who will listen and accept it from Him – not just the Jewish people to which He came as their long awaited Messiah. Jesus came for everyone to have their spiritual thirst quenched.

Draw near to Him today, open up your heart and your mind to Him and allow His spiritual water to fill you through prayer and studying His Word, then rest in the assurance that His eternal peace awaits us at the end of our journey here on earth.

Prayer

Dearest Lord Jesus, thank You for Your life-giving, spiritual water that You offer to all who will accept it. Fill us and quench our thirst for You and help us to rest in the assurance of Your eternal peace. Amen.

Finding God's Delight

Thus says the LORD:
Do not let the wise boast in their wisdom,
do not let the mighty boast in their might,
do not let the wealthy boast in their wealth;
but let those who boast boast in this,
that they understand and know me, that I am the LORD;
I act with steadfast love, justice,
and righteousness in the earth,
for in these things I delight, says the LORD.
~ Jeremiah 9:23-24

We all like to take pride in what we do. Some like to be acknowledged constantly for how much they know, how physically strong they are or how much they earn. Some are content to "do their thing" and not worry about the accolades that others crave in life. But what really matters to God?

God wants us to put Him first in our lives. If we are to seek knowledge and wisdom, we are to do so through His Word – not all of the human resources around us. The knowledge and wisdom we can glean from the past are all there in the Bible. The wealth we need to gain is this very knowledge available at our fingertips. We are to seek justice for those around us and to do the "right thing" in God's eyes – not necessarily what others around us may feel we should do. Like part of the lyrics from the song "Courageous" by Casting Crowns, we are to "Seek justice, Love mercy, Walk humbly with your God." This is what God wants from us.

Are you ready to spend more time seeking to know God better and to serve Him by seeking the justice lacking in society today? Are you ready to do the "right thing" in God's eyes? Now is the time to answer His call to action. He's watching and waiting for you to do just that.

Prayer

Lord on High, we so often forget to put You and Your will before our own. Things around us seem to pull us away from the close relationship we so desire with You. Help us, Lord, to return to putting You first in our lives. Help us to seek the justice that is lacking in the world around us; love the forgiveness that not only You give us, but that we extend to those around us; and to fall back into step with You as we humbly walk the path You desire for us to take through this life You have given us. Amen.

THE LOST IS FOUND

'Or what woman having ten silver coins,
if she loses one of them,
does not light a lamp, sweep the house,
and search carefully until she finds it?
*~ **Luke 15:8***

It was one of the coldest day we had had one winter and I had a text from my husband that his car wouldn't start when he went to leave for home. I left the church KNOWING I had my church keys, picked him up at his workplace and took him home. He had a basketball game later that night, so he took the van and I stayed home.

The next morning, as was my habit before leaving for work, I went to put my keys in my pocket, but they were GONE!!! I couldn't find them anywhere! I thought perhaps I was mistaken and had left them at work. I called the pastor and asked her to let me into the church when I got there. Bless her soul, she came running in the extreme cold to let me in. My search there was futile!

I looked again at home, more thoroughly and then again at the church that same evening before a meeting – no luck! Over the next several days I went over and over everywhere they could have been. I had a dream two days ago that the keys were found in a very obvious place that I had searched before. Finally, after almost two weeks, when I was finishing up my laundry, I searched to make sure I had everything out of the soak sink and there they were – THE KEYS!!! I praised God for letting me finally find them!

This must be how God feels when we wander away from Him. He looks and looks for us to find our way back, and sometimes He has to wait awhile for us to come to our senses and find our way back when we have taken a wrong turn in our lives. He and His angels rejoice with great excitement and singing when we return to God! It is one giant party when the lost are found!

Prayer

Dear Father in Heaven, thank you for loving us and always looking for us when we become lost. It is such a wonderful feeling that our returning to You brings You and your heavenly angels such joy! Please, help keep us on the right path with You so we no longer stray in our own directions so that we can continue to bring You great joy as we serve You. Amen.

Planted by Water

They shall be like a tree planted by water,
sending out its roots by the stream.
It shall not fear when heat comes,
and its leaves shall stay green;
in the year of drought it is not anxious,
and it does not cease to bear fruit.
~ Jeremiah 17:8

Oh my! Another scorcher day! The weatherman said we would reach as high as 95° F with a heat index of 105° F! Summer was definitely in full swing and we tend to plan our days around the worst of the heat. Most of us plan to stay in the air-conditioning at the worst part of the day and only traipse outside to do what we must and drink plenty of water to stay hydrated. There are those, though that do not have the luxury of air-conditioning; the homeless, the traveler whose vehicle's air-conditioning has malfunctioned, the poor that cannot afford the electricity to run their air or even possess an air-conditioner. Shelters for heat like this are sometimes available, but even then, not everyone who needs this relief is able to access it.

Our spiritual lives can be compared to surviving hot days such as these. Those that do not make time to spend with God on a daily basis through prayer, reading His Word and meditating on its meaning are like the un-watered plants in the extreme heat. They are more likely to wilt under the pressures of life and unwanted circumstances than someone that has partaken of the daily relationship with God and "drunk in" His Word. Those who make the time to delve into God's Word daily to "drink" from it the knowledge and life that He has supplied through this heavenly gift are better able to withstand the heat of difficult times and circumstances that come their way. They are like the trees planted by water - more able to gain the strength needed to withstand the extreme "heat" of life from daily Biblical nourishment and prayer to survive the turbulent times in their lives. They are able to not only survive severe circumstances, but also continue to do God's will and do not fear their situations, for they know that God is not only with them, but will continue to give them the strength they need.

Have you planted yourself by the "water of God's Word?" If not, "pull up your roots" and "replant yourself" where you will be most able to survive all that life may bring your way. By doing so, may you feel the life-giving water of God flowing through you – returning your strength to do His will and to survive all that life throws your way.

Prayer

Heavenly Father, life is full of unwanted circumstances and stresses beyond our control, yet, by the power of Your Word and by constantly being in communication with You through prayer, You "water" our lives with the life-giving strength to carry on in every situation that comes before us. We thank You for Your steadfast love and constant supervision as You nourish us through Your Word and guide us through this life You have given us. Amen.

Positives Vs. Negatives

*For what the flesh desires is opposed to the Spirit,
and what the Spirit desires is opposed to the flesh;
for these are opposed to each other, to prevent you from
doing what you want. But if you are led by the Spirit,
you are not subject to the law.
Now the works of the flesh are obvious:
fornication, impurity, licentiousness, idolatry, sorcery,
enmities, strife, jealousy, anger, quarrels, dissensions,
factions, envy, drunkenness, carousing, and things like these.
I am warning you, as I warned you before: those who do
such things will not inherit the kingdom of God.*

*By contrast, the fruit of the Spirit is love, joy, peace,
patience, kindness, generosity, faithfulness, gentleness, and
self-control. There is no law against such things.
And those who belong to Christ Jesus
have crucified the flesh with its passions and desires.
If we live by the Spirit, let us also be guided by the Spirit.
Let us not become conceited,
competing against one another, envying one another.*
~ *Galatians 5:17-26*

Some of us are positive people and some of us are negative. Some dwell on the negatives around them, while others tend to look at the brighter side of life. Being negative can drag not only ourselves down, but also those around us. By being positive, we can lift not only our own spirit, but also the spirits of those around us. The way we approach life can bring about happiness or sadness just by how we tend to look at things.

God tells us of the negative and positive attributes that are in this world. If we are led by His Spirit, we stay away from the negative attributes and seek the fruits of the Spirit for a happier, more fulfilling life. The choice is ours to make. By living by the fruits of the Spirit, we cannot commit sin, for there is no law saying that we will be punished by God for living out our lives with love, joy, peace, patience, kindness, generosity, faithfulness, gentleness and self-control. These look so much more appealing when looking at them in this light.

When we look at just one or two of the "sinful" attributes, we may think that perhaps partaking in a few of the lesser ones once or twice won't hurt. It almost makes us feel "dirty" to even consider partaking in these forbidden things when reading them all listed here in this passage, though. When we see some of what we may feel are "minor" negatives listed with the more severe by our standards, we see them all for what they really are – not worth even considering if we want to live a happy, God-filled life.

By belonging to Christ, we have given our lives over to Him – giving up our earthly passions and desires. We no longer want to live by the ways of which God has laws against, but rather, we strive to live as God wishes us to live. Let us change out any of our "bad fruit" from our lives and refill them with more "fruits of the Spirit." By doing this, we will live our lives more contentedly, knowing that we are pleasing God instead of momentarily pleasing ourselves.

Prayer

Father in Heaven, help us to look to You and Your Spirit to help us live according to the "positives" in life, so that all of our days may be filled with happiness in serving You. Amen.

FROM GENERATION TO GENERATION

He established a decree in Jacob,
and appointed a law in Israel,
which he commanded our ancestors
to teach to their children;
that the next generation might know them,
the children yet unborn,
and rise up and tell them to their children,
so that they should set their hope in God,
and not forget the works of God, but keep his
commandments;
*~ **Psalm 78:5-7***

We had just received the proof of the new photo directory that we hoped to have in hand as a final edition within a month! What a joy it was to see so many of the families that took the time to have their photo taken to be included. This was not only for current use, but would become a part of our historical archives in years to come. Our children and their children after them will be able to access this current church family's history as they look back at their former generations of worshipers here in this house of God and either remember us with love, or wonder what we were like back then. The one thing that they will know, though, is that this was a faithful congregation that chose to love God and pass that love on to the future generations by teaching them of God and His wonderful love for us all.

Way back when, even before Jesus, the Israelites were commanded by God through a decree in Jacob that they were to teach their children and have their children teach their children and on down the line so that future generations would know what God had done for them. By teaching them of God's faithfulness to them, they were helping future generations to set their hope in God and continue to follow His commandments. The future generations were able to learn of their history and all that God had done to preserve them as His chosen people, because of how much He loved them through this following this command.

What are we teaching our children? How are we passing on our faith to them? How can we improve in sharing this faith with future generations? It's time to really think about what and how we are doing this so that we also follow this command from God.

Prayer

Lord, thank you for all of those faithful ancestors before us that have handed down their faith in You to us. Help us to also hand our faith down to future generations to the best of our abilities so that our children and their children will also come to know You and faithfully serve You. Amen.

DANGER BEHIND THE BEAUTY

Therefore thus says the Lord GOD:
Because you have uttered falsehood and prophesied lies,
I am against you, says the Lord GOD.
My hand will be against the prophets who see false visions
and utter lying divinations; they shall not be in the council
of my people, nor be enrolled in the register of the house of
Israel, nor shall they enter the land of Israel;
and you shall know that I am the Lord GOD.
Because, in truth, because they have misled my people,
saying, 'Peace', when there is no peace;
and because, when the people build a wall,
these prophets smear whitewash on it. Say to those who
smear whitewash on it that it shall fall.
There will be a deluge of rain, great hailstones will fall,
and a stormy wind will break out.
When the wall falls, will it not be said to you, '
Where is the whitewash you smeared on it? '
~ Ezekiel 13:8-12

I had gone to Niagara Falls and found the beauty breathtaking! Standing next to the Horseshoe Falls, I could see the aqua-colored water running off of the edge of the rock, but if I looked closer, that rock was not a solid face downward. It is a thin layer that has slowly been undermined by the power of the water churning at the base of the cliff. Eventually, that rock will break away and the falls will retreat backward to a new ledge. What I once thought was a shear face of rock underneath that beautiful falling water is really a very precariously perched layer of rock with nothing under it for over a hundred feet below!

For many that do not study God's word diligently, they may believe whatever false teachers and religious leaders with hidden agendas say, for they do not have a solid base of knowledge about God. False teachers are all around us in this world, trying to lead us away from God and the way God truly wants us to live our lives. If we do not study God's Word ourselves and instead believe everything we hear from others, we may be like that waterfall – our faith life may seem good on the outside, but we are being undermined by the power of false teachings that will eventually cause us to fall away from the faith God wants us to have in Him. We must not only listen to the teachings of God, but also be able to compare those teaching against what we have learned from our own Bible study to be sure that what we are hearing is true and sound, for if we do not guard against false teachings, we may find ourselves breaking off from the faith we so dearly want to hang on to and falling to a certain death in the churning waters of confusion and despair.

Build up your Christian foundation by building the necessary supports of the knowledge of God and His Word underneath you so that you can better discern who is teaching truth and who is trying to lead you away from God. It's never too late to crack open your Bible and start learning!

Prayer

Dear Lord, we thank you for Your Word that we can study and refer to when we become confused about teachings that we are told are from You. You have given us a very great treasure in Your Word by allowing us to use it as a guide to discern who is teaching according to Your will and those who are trying to lead us away from You. Help us all to make the time to read and study Your Word daily, so that we can build firm foundations from which our faith can grow, not fall away. Amen.

LEARNING TO LOVE

We love because he first loved us. Those who say,
'I love God', and hate their brothers or sisters, are liars;
for those who do not love a brother or sister
whom they have seen,
cannot love God whom they have not seen.
The commandment we have from him is this:
those who love God
must love their brothers and sisters also.
~ 1 John 5:19-21

How many of us have no one we dislike? I'm sure that almost everyone can name at least one person who they cannot stand to be around. Is this how we, as Christians, are to act? We often hear the words, "I hate so-and-so!" Hate is not of God, though, so if we cannot find it in our hearts to learn to love even the most difficult to love, how can we love God?

God created us because He is love. Love has to have someone to share that love with. God cannot hate, because He is love.

If we cannot love everyone (yes, this can be very difficult at times), we cannot love God. We must learn to find something to love about each person. Everyone must have some redeeming quality. True, there are those that are so very evil that we think that there cannot be anything good in them, yet God still loves them and yearns for them to return to Him, so there must be something there to love. We just really need to look hard at what that something might be. By learning to love everyone, we can finally love God as well. How else can we love something unseen when we cannot love everyone He has created to love that we can see?

Prayer

Dear Lord, thank You for Your constant love, even when we know we don't deserve it. Help us to love everyone as You do, so that we can love You as You wish us to love. Amen.

Hope in Difficult Times

The steadfast love of the LORD never ceases,
his mercies never come to an end;
they are new every morning;
great is your faithfulness.
'The LORD is my portion,' says my soul,
'therefore I will hope in him.'
*~ **Lamentations 3:22-24***

There are days when we hear news that saddens us. The fact that someone is ill, a family is going through difficult times, or someone has lost someone dear to them can take the wind out of us when we also share a relationship with that person or family. We want so much to step in and do something to show them that we care and are there for them to lean on.

God can use us every day to help show His never ending love for others. He has used those that love Him repeatedly over the centuries to do just that. Prophets pointed the way back to God when Israel had gone astray. Moses led the people out of Egypt after 400 years of slavery. Jesus died on the cross and rose again to conquer death and sin to give us a way to salvation through Him so that we could have eternal life with God.

God has never abandoned us – not even in our darkest hours. He has always been there for us when we call on His name. Reach out to Him now. He is the one in whom we hope and will always help us in our time of need. In turn, we need to allow Him to work through us to show His love to others every day, so that they may also put their hope in Him.

Prayer

Lord, we know that there are difficult days in our lives as well as good days. Thank You for always being there for us to lean on in times of trouble. Use us to help others to find you and put their hope and trust in You also. Amen.

LASTING IMPRESSIONS

Come now, you who say,
'Today or tomorrow we will go to such and such a town
and spend a year there,
doing business and making money.'
Yet you do not even know what tomorrow will bring.
What is your life?
For you are a mist that appears for a little while
and then vanishes.
Instead you ought to say,
'If the Lord wishes, we will live and do this or that.
'As it is, you boast in your arrogance;
all such boasting is evil.
Anyone, then, who knows the right thing to do
and fails to do it, commits sin.
*~ **James 4:13-17***

I stepped out into the mist and was reminded that we, too are so like this very mist. A mist, unlike a heavy rain, leaves a light film of moisture that may or may not soak into the soil ever so slightly before evaporating back into the atmosphere. Our lives, in comparison to God and His eternalness, also lightly touch the earth and those around us while we are here. Some of us leave a lasting impression as our accomplishments may sink into society and be associated with our name for many years after we are gone, but most of us are here and leave this earth without leaving much of an impression – like the mist – except for on the family and friends around us. Once we are gone, we may be forgotten in time to this earth.

Procrastination is one of those traits that keep us from leaving an impression on those around us. By putting off today what we feel we can do tomorrow, or next week, we may be losing the very opportunity to make that lasting impression God has put us here to make. Waiting to tell someone you love them, or about Christ and His love for them may not wait another moment. It is up to God how long we are here, not us, so we need to make the most out of each moment of our lives if we wish to please Him. We are being arrogant to think that God will keep us here another moment. It is His will that we live right now. We do not know what He has planned for us tomorrow. Let's not wait and waste our time here today. We need to use our time wisely – as if this is the only moment left in our life to do God's will in spreading His love and message to others.

Prayer

Heavenly Father, we are but a mist in time here. Please, help us to use our time wisely to further Your kingdom and love for others. Amen.

WHERE ARE OUR PRIORITIES?

There is an evil that I have seen under the sun,
and it lies heavy upon humankind:
those to whom God gives wealth, possessions, and honor,
so that they lack nothing of all that they desire,
yet God does not enable them to enjoy these things,
but a stranger enjoys them. This is vanity; it is a grievous ill.
A man may beget a hundred children,
and live for many years;
but however many are the days of his years,
if he does not enjoy life's good things, or has no burial,
I say that a stillborn child is better off than he.
~ Ecclesiastes 6:1-3

The son of a couple I graduated with from high school had made a very important decision in his life – one that is very honorable in many people's eyes. This son of theirs was a professional football player that had just won the Super Bowl earlier that year. He had the choice of signing a one-year un-guaranteed contract or retire. He had only played professional ball for 9 years, so in reality, he could have continued playing, but he consulted his wife and made the decision to retire. He felt he was missing out on too much of his four young children's lives and would rather spend time being a father to them than making the hundreds of thousands of dollars he could have made by signing the contract.

So often in society today, people choose money over what is really important in life – the love of God and family. God will always bless those that make the right decisions according to His will. He never says life will be easy when we choose to follow His ways, but He will bless us for doing His will above our own. There are those that do struggle financially to make ends meet, but all God really is looking for any one of us to do is to make our priorities in life according to what He says they should be. If we put God first, family second and others ahead of ourselves, we will be rewarded with blessings from God that we cannot even imagine down the road.

Where do your priorities lie? Are you putting God first? Do you need to make some changes? Now is never too late!

Prayer

Dear Lord in Heaven, there are so many temptations around us to build up earthly treasures. Keep us grounded to what Your will in our lives is and what is most important in life. May we re-prioritize our lives where it needs to be made more in line with Your will so that we are truly living as You wish us to live – serving You and others in this world. Amen.

What Lies Beyond?

Then I heard what seemed to be the voice
of a great multitude, like the sound of many waters
and like the sound of mighty thunder-peals, crying out,
'Hallelujah!
For the Lord our God
the Almighty reigns.
~ Revelation 19:6

Many years ago, when my grandmother had passed away from cancer, I remember my mother saying that she no longer feared death. While she had been watching at her mother's bedside as her mother's last hours on this earth neared, her mother woke up and asked her who was singing in the hallway of the hospital. My mother said there were some nurses in the hall talking, but no one was singing. Her mother insisted that, no, it wasn't talking she heard, but singing.

A couple of hours later, after my aunt had relieved my mother of the bedside vigil, my grandmother opened her eyes from her sleep, looked to the window as if she saw something and followed her gaze up toward the ceiling. My aunt, wondering what her mother was looking at, looked up to see what my grandmother might have been so intently looking at. Seeing nothing, she looked back at her mother and she had passed from this world to the next.

God gives us glimpses in scripture many times over of what lies beyond this life. Those that are already in heaven will be shouting, singing and praising God! A great celebration of eternal life with our glorious Heavenly Father is what is awaiting us! We need not fear our earthly death, for it leads to an eternal life for those of us who believe in Him and have repented of our sins through the blood of His Son, Jesus Christ.

Prayer

Father in Heaven, we thank you for these glimpses of heaven that you show us, not only in the Bible, but in the last moments of those we love as they pass from this world to Your eternal peace so that we who believe no longer need to fear what lies beyond this life. Amen.

THE FINISH LINE

I have fought the good fight, I have finished the race,
I have kept the faith.
From now on there is reserved for me
the crown of righteousness,
which the Lord, the righteous judge,
will give to me on that day,
and not only to me but also to all
who have longed for his appearing.
~ 2 Timothy 4:7-8

I have never run more than a mile at a time in my life – and that was back in high school gym class and only because it was required. I usually prefer to joke about how I am allergic to exercise – it makes me break out in a sweat! When I was required to run, there was always the voice telling me to slow down and walk a little bit, but if I had stopped, it would have been harder to get going again. Ignoring that voice and listening instead to the pace of foot falls of a fellow classmate that was on the track team, I was able to stay ahead and run the entire mile without stopping. Granted, I would walk it off a little bit so that I wouldn't cramp up and then would lie down on the gym floor or in the grass, depending on if we were inside or out, and try to catch my breath again.

The Christian life is much like running a race. We must diligently set aside time and study scripture and pray in order to build up the strength and endurance to run this race we call life instead of just getting up and settling back into our own routine for the day. We cannot get lazy and break our pace of reading and prayer or it becomes that much harder to get back into a routine of faithful communing with God. We will be rewarded at the end of our lives for our faithfulness to Him, as we not only study and pray, but apply what we learn from God in our daily lives to live more like Christ.

Prayer

Dear Lord, help us to set aside some time each day to study and pray to You so that we can finish this race called life by crossing the finish line living our lives as Christ would have us live. Amen.

WITH OUR WHOLE HEART

For this reason I bow my knees before the Father,
from whom every family in heaven
and on earth takes its name.
I pray that, according to the riches of his glory,
he may grant that you may be strengthened in your inner
being with power through his Spirit,
and that Christ may dwell in your hearts through faith,
as you are being rooted and grounded in love.
I pray that you may have the power to comprehend,
with all the saints,
what is the breadth and length and height and depth,
and to know the love of Christ that surpasses knowledge,
so that you may be filled with all the fullness of God.
*~ **Ephesians 3:14-19***

As a small child, I remember trying to explain to my mom one day just how much I loved her. I loved her with my WHOLE heart! Even that seemed like not enough of an explanation for how I felt about her and how she did her all to make my childhood a happy one.

Christ loves us, too. Paul prays that we might be able to wrap our mind around just how much Christ loves us. To imagine an infinite length, height and depth of His love is still unimaginable to our minds, but because of this immense love for us, He died for us to save us from our sin and inevitable death. Just reading this explanation of love can make our hearts swell with our love and appreciation for Jesus. It should make us all want to drop to our knees in praise and thanksgiving to Him for all He has done to give us a way to eternal life.

How much do you love Christ? Do you love Him with your whole heart? Remember to thank and praise Him for all He has done for you. He would LOVE to hear from you!

Prayer

Dearest Lord Jesus, we thank you for the un-comprehendible amount of love You have for us. We thank You for Your ultimate sacrifice so that we may one day be with You for all eternity. Amen.

PROCLAIMING THE MESSAGE

In the presence of God and of Christ Jesus,
who is to judge the living and the dead,
and in view of his appearing and his kingdom,
I solemnly urge you: proclaim the message;
be persistent whether the time is favorable or unfavorable;
convince, rebuke, and encourage,
with the utmost patience in teaching.
For the time is coming when people
will not put up with sound doctrine,
but having itching ears, they will accumulate for themselves
teachers to suit their own desires,
and will turn away from listening to the truth
and wander away to myths.
~ 2 Timothy 4:1-4

How many times as a child did you ask a parent for something, and having been told "no," went to the other parent asking the same question and hoping for a different answer? How many of us greatly dislike being told what we are doing is wrong and prefers to find others that do agree with what we are doing? It's only human nature to want to do things our own way and have what we are doing be considered the correct thing to do in any given situation.

Even today, people change faiths and churches so that they surround themselves with those that believe as they do instead of having to adjust the way they believe to what is being taught. People interpret the Bible differently than they did years ago, taking things out of context and applying their own way of thinking to twist the meanings of what the scriptures are teaching us and then teach others based on their own interpretation of the Bible. Those that do not study the Word of God on their own and trust what others are telling them are often led away from what the true meaning behind the scriptures really is.

It is up to each one of us to study the Holy Word of God on our own, so that we know personally what He instructs us to do and can shy away from the false teachings that are out there today. We must not be shy in relating what the true meaning in the scriptures is when others try to tell us their false interpretations that they may have heard from someone else with their own agenda, so that we can put them back on the right track of what God is truly wanting us to learn from His Word. God is the same as He was in the beginning and will continue to be for eternity. His Word does not change, so we should not try to change it to fit our own agendas. God's message has been the same since the beginning of time. We are to love Him with our whole being, putting Him first above all else. Then we are to love others and treat them as we wish to be treated. It's that simple.

We can love the sinner, but hate the sin, as we have heard many times in the past. Even Jesus ate with sinners, so we can commune with them as well while we try to lead them back to a Christian way of life. The Bible doesn't say that we are to find a way to adjust God's Word to fit the sinner so that their way of life can continue. We are not to condemn people for their way of life either, for it is not for us to judge. However, we can instruct them in the way God wants them to live and tell them that they can receive forgiveness if they repent and turn from their sinful ways. As Jesus told the prostitute after He saved her from being stoned by the scribes and Pharisees, "Neither do I condemn you. Go your way, and from now on do not sin again." (John 8:11)

Prayer

Dear Lord Jesus, help us to interpret Your Word correctly, without putting our own personal spin or agenda into it, so that we learn from it what it is You have wanted us to learn since the beginning of time. Help us to correct others when they relate incorrect interpretations that they may have heard so that they will be set straight and not be led astray by false teachings. Let us not judge others, for that is for You to do. Instead, help us to lead others to follow You as You wish everyone to do and stay faithful to You until we meet in Your Heavenly Kingdom. Amen.

NEVER ALONE

The LORD answer you in the day of trouble!
The name of the God of Jacob protect you!
May he send you help from the sanctuary,
and give you support from Zion.
*~ **Psalm 20:1-2***

We occasionally have those days when nothing seems to go right. The computer is not working properly, you misplace your keys, a "wardrobe malfunction" occurs after you have arrived at your destination... These are, of course, all minor in comparison to what some people must face on a daily basis - homelessness, health issues, hunger...

No matter what may befall you, our Lord will be there for you. Just call on Him and He will be there to help you - to calm your nerves and wrap you in His arms to give you strength and peace through difficult times. The help you request may not be answered with a solution to all of your problems, but you will never have to face your troubles alone. God will never put you through more than you and He together can't handle.

Prayer

Lord, thank you for always walking by my side - helping me through whatever comes my way, be it small problems or difficult circumstances. I know that, with You, all things can be overcome in time. Amen.

GIVING IT YOUR ALL

Do nothing from selfish ambition or conceit,
but in humility regard others as better than yourselves.
Let each of you look not to your own interests,
but to the interests of others.
Let the same mind be in you that was in Christ Jesus,
who, though he was in the form of God,
did not regard equality with God
as something to be exploited,
but emptied himself, taking the form of a slave,
being born in human likeness.
And being found in human form, he humbled himself
and became obedient to the point of death—
even death on a cross.
*~ **Philippians 2:3-8***

Have you ever seen someone that loves to pat themselves on the back and let everyone know what they have done and why? Most of us have seen people like that, but we sometimes tend to have a lesser view of them when they brag about their accomplishments. Sometimes it appears that they do what they do for accolades from others instead of doing things from the heart for others.

Paul writes about this to the Philippians. We are not to do things so that others can praise us for our accomplishments or feel that we are better than someone else. Instead, we are to be more like Christ, who was obedient to the Father by leaving paradise to be one of the lowly among the earth. He served others out of love for the Father – not for accolades from others for Himself, but to bring glory to God.

This is just the attitude in which we are also to serve others – to bring glory to our Father in heaven, not to ourselves. We are to serve Him humbly, as Christ also served on this earth. By remaining humble, we allow God to receive the glory He deserves. This helps point the way to others that we serve that what we do, we do for God and not ourselves. In this manner of service, we may lead others to see God's grace and glory as well.

What are you doing to show others God's love in this world? Are you helping to point the way to our Heavenly Father? Give it your all when serving Him. Allow God's love to touch others around you without seeking praise for yourself. By serving in this way, your efforts bring praises to God by those you serve.

Prayer

Dearest Lord Jesus, help us to do all things for your glory, not our own, so that our service to others helps lead them to You. Amen.

"Cut It Off" and Find Peace

If your right eye causes you to sin,
tear it out and throw it away;
it is better for you to lose one of your members
than for your whole body to be thrown into hell.
And if your right hand causes you to sin,
cut it off and throw it away;
it is better for you to lose one of your members
than for your whole body to go into hell.
*~ **Matthew 5:29-30***

Jesus told a crowd of followers and curious people that if a part of their body caused them to sin, they were to "tear it out" or "cut it off!" Seems pretty drastic to anyone listening. Did Jesus really mean to do just that? Probably not. Jesus often spoke figuratively when trying to get a point across.

What Jesus was trying to get at is that if there is something in your life that habitually leads you to sin – get rid of that "thing" to keep from sinning. If you have an alcohol problem, don't hang around in bars or places that serve alcohol. If you have "friends" with bad habits that rub off on you, don't "hang" with those friends – find new ones that don't have those particular habits. If certain printed material, websites or movies create sinful urges – don't waste your time looking at them. Find things and people to be around that will not tend to lead you to places that draw you into sin. You will find that your life will become much happier when you fill your life with the good things and good people that God wants you to fill your life with than to continually follow down a sinful path that will never fulfill you with the love and peace that Christ has to offer.

Do you have habits that need to be removed from your life to get closer to God? What can you do to remove them? Start today to find a better path that will lead you to the peace and happiness Christ has waiting for you!

Prayer

Dear Jesus, we are such weak creatures when it comes to sinfulness. Help us to remove the things in our lives that lead us away from You so that we can find the love and peace waiting for us when we follow You. Amen.

Keeping Up with the Joneses

Of course, there is great gain in godliness
combined with contentment;
for we brought nothing into the world,
so that we can take nothing out of it;
but if we have food and clothing,
we will be content with these.
But those who want to be rich fall into temptation
and are trapped by many senseless and harmful desires
that plunge people into ruin and destruction.
For the love of money is a root of all kinds of evil,
and in their eagerness to be rich
some have wandered away from the faith
and pierced themselves with many pains.
~ 1 Timothy 6:6-10

"Keeping up with the Joneses" is a phrase I learned as a child when hearing my parents speak about someone we knew who always had to have the biggest or most expensive items in the neighborhood. If someone got a new riding lawnmower, within a few weeks this particular neighbor would have a newer, bigger and better one. People with money are not always like this, but sometimes they don't know what else to do with their money, so they have a tendency to "out-do" the possessions of those around them to show their financial status.

Sometimes, "keeping up with the Joneses" can put those that do not have a lot of money in financial straits, because even though they really can't afford something, they want everyone around them to think they can. They overspend their income by taking out loans to a point that they are in debt way over their heads. The next thing they know, they have to declare bankruptcy and end up losing everything they had. This becomes very embarrassing for them.

Of course, there are also those that have money and handle this gift from God very wisely; becoming benefactors to many organizations that help those that are less fortunate. They are not driven by their desire for everyone to see just how much they have. They realize that what they have is a gift and that it is not something that should be squandered foolishly on things that do not last or just to impress others. They are considered good stewards of what God has so graciously allowed them to have in this life here on earth.

The love of money has been a stumbling block for many for centuries. It can become an all-consuming fire for some of us that pulls us away from our faith and love of God, who provides us with all we have. Money can also be a great gift that can be judiciously handled to benefit others. The best thing to do with our gifts from God, whether it be money or talents, is to give them back to God as an offering. We need to prayerfully consider all God has given us and then offer whatever He has given us back to Him to be used for His glory. God will bless these gifts to Him abundantly - bringing us peace and contentment in this life, as opposed to all of the problems that these gifts can bring if they are hung onto for ourselves.

Prayer

Heavenly Father, thank You for the many gifts You have given us. We ask that You allow us to return these gifts to You so that they may be used to further Your kingdom. Amen.

ONE OF THOSE DAYS...

Jesus departed with his disciples to the lake,
and a great multitude from Galilee followed him;
hearing all that he was doing,
they came to him in great numbers from Judea,
Jerusalem, Idumea,
beyond the Jordan, and the region around Tyre and Sidon.
He told his disciples to have a boat ready for him
because of the crowd,
so that they would not crush him; for he had cured many,
so that all who had diseases pressed upon him to touch him.
Whenever the unclean spirits saw him,
they fell down before him and shouted,
'You are the Son of God!'
But he sternly ordered them not to make him known.
*~ **Mark 3:7-12***

Have you ever had "one of those days" where you are pulled every which way but the way you were wanting to head? I have those frequently. No two days are alike. To have a day where everything goes as planned is rare - far and few between.

Jesus must have felt that way often as we read through the Gospels of Matthew, Mark, Luke and John. Once news of His teachings and miraculous healings got out, it was very difficult for Him to find some "alone" time. Much like our celebrities of today, people mobbed Him to hear Him speak or to see if they could be the object of one of His miracles in healing.

Jesus' disciples knew who Jesus really was, but Jesus even ordered the unclean spirits to keep that secret. Jesus didn't want that to be made public at the time. Why, we may ask? It may have been because He was fully human AND fully divine, yet had not completed what He had set out to do while here in human form. What would have happened had He allowed who He really was to made known to all who would listen BEFORE He had died on the cross and risen again? Would His mission have turned out differently? Had enough people believed He was the promised Messiah, would they have allowed Him to be crucified? How many innocent lives may have been lost by those that did believe He was the Messiah being killed by those that did not believe before Jesus was able to complete His mission? We will never know the answer for sure until we reach heaven one day.

All we do know from this scripture for sure is that, even though we may have "one of those days" here and there, Jesus had a lot of them as well. He was able to get through them by pulling Himself away from the crowds to have alone time with His Heavenly Father to bring Himself back to where he needed to be spiritually (Matthew 26:36). We can do this very same thing. On days like these, it is important to "pull away" and center our lives back in unity with God, so that He can give our minds and hearts the peace we so disparately need to "keep on keeping on."

Prayer

Dear Lord Jesus, help us to follow Your example of meeting the needs that God wants us to fulfill and to know when to say it is time to meet with God for a little "one-on-one" time with Him to help keep us sane on the days that we feel we can't possibly meet all of the demands of those around us. Amen.

Body Transplant

For we know that if the earthly tent we live in is destroyed,
we have a building from God, a house not made with hands,
eternal in the heavens. For in this tent we groan,
longing to be clothed with our heavenly dwelling—
if indeed, when we have taken it off
we will not be found naked.
For while we are still in this tent,
we groan under our burden,
because we wish not to be unclothed
but to be further clothed,
so that what is mortal may be swallowed up by life.
He who has prepared us for this very thing is God,
who has given us the Spirit as a guarantee.

So we are always confident; even though we know that
while we are at home in the body we are away from the
Lord— for we walk by faith, not by sight.
Yes, we do have confidence,
and we would rather be away from the body and at home
with the Lord. So whether we are at home or away, we
make it our aim to please him. For all of us must appear
before the judgment seat of Christ, so that each may receive
recompense for what has been done in the body,
whether good or evil.
*~ **2 Corinthians 5:1-21***

I often joke about wanting a body transplant ~ a younger model with a better shape and less weight. I often see and hear others that are unhappy with their earthly bodies as well. The aches and pains of getting older are felt with each progressing year.

Paul tells us that we are living in an "earthly tent" when here on earth. God has an eternal home - a heavenly body - waiting for us one day that will not have all of the issues our current bodies must bear. We moan and groan under all that we must deal with while here on earth, but one day, we know that our spirit will "shed" this body and take on its heavenly body when we go to be with our Lord and Savior. We walk in faith that this is so, for we cannot see it while here on earth, but know that God has it waiting for us, because Jesus has told us so.

We also will have to account for what we have done while here on earth in our earthly bodies. Although we cannot "earn" our way to heaven, for it is the gift of Jesus' saving grace by which we may enter heaven, we do need to live our earthly lives as Christ would have us live - serving Him and others out of our love of Him and gratitude for His amazing gift. This heavenly "body transplant" is waiting for us one day, where we will claim it at Jesus' judgment seat when He tells us "well done, good and faithful servant." Are we living as Christ would have us live? Or must we make some adjustments to live more like Him while we still can?

Prayer

Dear Lord, we thank You, that You have a "body transplant" waiting with our name on it there in heaven with You. Help us to live out our earthly lives here showing the love and gratitude for Your amazing gift You have waiting for us one day. Amen.

GATHERING TOGETHER

For I am longing to see you
so that I may share with you some spiritual gift
to strengthen you—
or rather so that we may be mutually encouraged
by each other's faith, both yours and mine.
~ Romans 1:11-12

When I was a child, my mother saw to it that we went to Sunday School every Sunday, often taking neighborhood kids with us as well. We would sometimes ask, "Why doesn't daddy come to church?" to which she would reply that he worked 6 days a week and needed to get some additional sleep. Dad's answer was that he would attend "TV church" when he got up. We would think this unfair - usually when it was extremely cold out and didn't really want to travel in the cold back and forth to church, but mom was always adamant that we go and dad always supported her in that as well. Dad did start attending many years later and was finally baptized, but until he started going to church, his faith was stagnant.

Paul explains in Romans that getting together to share our faith with each other is important for everyone involved. By sharing our faith with each other on a regular basis, we help reinforce and strengthen each other's faith as well. By sharing our spiritual gifts, we help each other grow in our spiritual lives, where staying alone with our faith may keep our faith stagnant or weaken it during difficult times when others of faith can help bolster our faith when we aren't sure of our own faith seeing us through difficult times alone.

Have you been attending church regularly? If not, what is holding you back? Make a point to get together with your church family in worship this Sunday. Enjoy fellowshipping together before and after service as well. Strengthen your faith ties with others of similar beliefs and watch your faith grow stronger.

Prayer

Dear Lord, thank You for allowing us places to gather with others that believe in You for our faith in You to be mutually strengthened. Help us to always make the greatest effort to attend faithfully instead of making excuses to miss a week so that our faith continues to grow. Amen.

A TIME FOR EVERYTHING

For everything there is a season,
and a time for every matter under heaven:
a time to be born, and a time to die;
a time to plant, and a time to pluck up what is planted;
a time to kill, and a time to heal;
a time to break down, and a time to build up;
a time to weep, and a time to laugh;
a time to mourn, and a time to dance;
a time to throw away stones,
and a time to gather stones together;
a time to embrace, and a time to refrain from embracing;
a time to seek, and a time to lose;
a time to keep, and a time to throw away;
a time to tear, and a time to sew;
a time to keep silence, and a time to speak;
a time to love, and a time to hate;
a time for war, and a time for peace.
~ Ecclesiastes 3

Looking out the window at the first signs of fall, I am reminded that each season is beautiful in its own way. Winter brings the beauty of the magically transformed world into one purified in white (at least until traffic and pollution turn it to a grayish-black "mush" along the roadways.) Spring shows the many colors of newly formed leaves in several shades of green just "popping" out of their buds and the few new spring flowers bursting through the ground to meet the sunshine each day. Summer has the deeper shades of green when the trees loan us their shade to keep the sun's heat at bay during the day, while fall shows us the many splendid colors of God's artist's palette.

Life is much like the seasons: the beauty of a newborn child in all of their soft purity and newness of life; the endless energy and care-free life of a child at play; the much busier "grown-up version" of adult life; and the frail bodies and wise minds of those "more seasoned in life" as they near their journey's end here on earth. Each season of life has it's own beauty in our eyes. We must approach life as we do the seasons each year - enjoying each as it lasts and looking for its beauty as we pass through them, for this is what God has created for us to enjoy. May we all find the beauty in our lives as we travel this earthly road towards heaven's gate someday in the future.

Prayer

Dear Lord, as we travel along life's road - however long or short our path here - may we always take the time to enjoy the beauty of the lives we are living here as we come closer to Your kingdom at the end of our path. Amen.

SUBTLE CHANGES

The words of the wise:
Incline your ear and hear my words,
and apply your mind to my teaching;
for it will be pleasant if you keep them within you,
if all of them are ready on your lips.
So that your trust may be in the Lord,
I have made them known to you today—yes, to you.
*~ **Proverbs 22:17-19***

Looking around you, you may not always notice that what you saw a moment ago is now a little different. Another leaf may have drifted down as you closed your eyes and you missed its fall, but it is now on the ground, where a moment ago, it was not. A bird may have been singing and has now stopped its melodic song. The cicada has gotten just a little louder than it was a moment ago.

God's Word has so much meaning hidden within it. What you read as a child may now hold a different meaning to you as you go through different trials in life. The same passage may help you through one trial and years later, help you through another much different trial in a slightly different way.

Saying that you have read the Bible cover to cover so you don't have to read it again is such a waste of eternal knowledge right at your fingertips. Keep studying God's Word daily - reading and re-reading it and meditating on it. Pray for His wisdom to speak to you through His Words so that you may apply this wisdom in your life right now. What you applied a moment ago may be different than what you will need in the next moment, based on where God is leading you at that time, so be in a constant search for His truth every day. He will reveal to you what He wishes you to know for the moment and this may be different than He revealed yesterday as well as what He will reveal tomorrow.

Prayer

Father, what a beautiful gift of wisdom You have given us. So often we take Your Word for granted and don't take the time to look for the deeper meaning You wish to reveal to us. Let us make the time to really study Your Word and listen for Your voice revealing what we are to learn and then apply it to our lives. Amen.

GOD'S WILL, NOT OUR OWN

And going a little farther,
he threw himself on the ground and prayed that,
if it were possible, the hour might pass from him.
He said, 'Abba, Father, for you all things are possible;
remove this cup from me; yet, not what I want,
but what you want.'
~ Mark 14:35-36

We have often heard that we are to pray when things seem hopeless or we are having difficult times. I have seen many prayers answered shortly after having been lifted up. Does this mean that we will receive everything we ask for? No. If that were so, there would be no jobless, no hunger, no homeless, no poor and on and on. Then why are we told to pray?

We pray and lift up our desires, problems and fears to God. Even though He already knows what we are thinking and feeling, it is our way to communicate to God and have a relationship with Him. He is our Heavenly Father, and like any parent, He will give us what we ask for IF He feels it is best for us. Sometimes, what we feel is best for us is not always the case. God has a much better plan for us. He may not let you have the sports car you have always desired, because He knows that the temptation to push the limit with it may be too great for you, endangering not only yourself, but others on the road. He may not heal you of your ailment, no matter how life-threatening it may be, because He has a greater plan for you in the end.

Jesus knew what was coming in the next day for Him as He pleaded with God to carry out His plan in another way, yet

Jesus also yielded to His Father's plan in faith that He would come out of all of the torture and death alive again - becoming the bridge to bring us all to eternal life one day with Him. Jesus went to the cross knowing that God would overcome whatever He faced at the moment. Three days later, Jesus conquered the grave and now reigns eternally with the Father. Are you willing to have the faith it takes to ask God for His will to be done in your life, no matter the sacrifices you may have to make? Can you carry on with whatever God has given you to deal with to fulfill His will in your life if He chooses not to remove what you would like to have removed? Will your faith in Him continue, even if you must continue to deal with whatever God has chosen for you to deal with here on earth? Continue to pray, but remember to also end your requests by letting God know that, even though you would like for Him to remove whatever it is that you don't want, to have His will - not your own - be done. You never know how much you will be blessed in the end, no matter what God's decision may be.

Prayer

Dear Heavenly Father, we know that all things are used by You for good. Help us to pray with faith in whatever Your decisions about our paths may be, knowing that, in the end, You will bless us for remaining faithful through whatever trials we must face. Amen.

AFFLICTION AND CONSOLATION

Blessed be the God and Father of our Lord Jesus Christ,
the Father of mercies and the God of all consolation,
who consoles us in all our affliction,
so that we may be able to console those
who are in any affliction
with the consolation with which we ourselves
are consoled by God.
~ 2 Corinthians 1:3-4

There is a day of remembrance of the lives lost during the 9/11 attack by terrorists in New York City, Washington D.C. and in a field in Pennsylvania. Those of us alive at that fateful time of 8:26 A.M. eastern time fully remember where we were and what we were doing when that first plane hit one of the twin towers in New York City, followed by the second plane, the third into the Pentagon and the fourth into a field (thanks to some heroes that took it upon themselves to save countless lives by sacrificing themselves to take the hijacker down before doing further damage to other highly populated or important areas on the ground. That evening, many churches were filled with mourners asking, "Why?" and searching to be consoled as the world as we knew it was no more.

Christ was there for those that lost their lives, as well as those mourning their loss. He suffered along with us at the senseless loss of life. Christ was, and still is, there to console those mourning the loss of friends, colleagues and family that were lost to us here on earth that day. Knowing that Christ not only shares in our sorrows and afflictions and consoles us allows us to have hope in Him that is unshaken, even in the face of some of the worst tragedies that can possibly assail us.

Christ continues to be there for you, now and in the future, to share anything that may come your way to try to shake your faith in Him. He will never leave or forsake you, so trust Him in all things to bring you safely through the dark times to brighter days ahead. Are you willing to hold fast to Him, no matter what may come your way?

Prayer

Dear Jesus, we thank You that You are always with us - sharing in our darkest hours as well as consoling us and carrying us to brighter days ahead. Help us to continue to hold tightly to our hope that is in You. Amen.

SHARE THE LOVE

For God is not unjust;
he will not overlook your work and the love that you showed
for his sake in serving the saints, as you still do.
And we want each one of you to show the same diligence,
so as to realize the full assurance of hope to the very end,
so that you may not become sluggish,
but imitators of those who
through faith and patience inherit the promises.
~ Hebrews 6:10-12

We have heard that you cannot "earn" your way to heaven. However, we also cannot sit idly by and "do nothing" to get to heaven, either. Then how do we gain entrance into heaven at the end of this life?

We must believe that Christ was the Messiah and Savior that died for our sins. We must repent of our own sins and try to live a Christ-like life and accept His gift of salvation, which is freely given to all who believe. We must imitate Christ and all those of faith that put others before themselves so that they will also come to know the love of Christ and our Heavenly Father.

Do we have to do amazing feats of service to gain our eternal home with Christ? No. We do, however, need to always be prepared to do what is needed at the moment to further God's kingdom here on earth. Share a listening ear to those who are hurting physically and spiritually. Feed those who are hungry. Clothe those that are in need of clothing. Do whatever you feel called at the moment to do to show God's love. Serve "at the drop of a hat" when you see a need arise. Share the love of Christ for which we are all called to do so that others may be saved for His kingdom by our service in His name.

Prayer

Dear Lord, here we are! Use us as You need to further Your kingdom. Thank You for Your gift of salvation, which is freely given to all who believe in You. Amen.

LIGHTING YOUR FAITH ON FIRE

'And to the angel of the church in Laodicea write:
The words of the Amen, the faithful and true witness,
the origin of God's creation:
'I know your works; you are neither cold nor hot.
I wish that you were either cold or hot.
So, because you are lukewarm, and neither cold nor hot,
I am about to spit you out of my mouth. For you say,
"I am rich, I have prospered, and I need nothing."
You do not realize that you are wretched, pitiable,
poor, blind, and naked.
Therefore I counsel you to buy from me gold refined by fire
so that you may be rich;
and white robes to clothe you
and to keep the shame of your nakedness from being seen;
and salve to anoint your eyes so that you may see.
I reprove and discipline those whom I love.
Be earnest, therefore, and repent.
*~ **Revelation 3:14-19***

As we come closer to the end of times, Revelation reminds us that we must not be "lukewarm" in our faith. In fact, according to Retha McPherson, who is co-author of a book "Messages from God," we are to light our faith on fire! I have ordered this book and am looking forward to reading more of what she and her son Aldo, have been inspired by God to write.

We often look at our lives and think that we are doing just fine as we are, including in our faith life. But are we really? How often do we speak of God to others? Or are we afraid of offending someone by talking about our faith? How often do we draw close to God and connect with Him in a relational conversation through prayer and meditation?

Revelation speaks to this very problem of being "hot" or "cold" in our faith by showing us that we need to get the very things we need for our faith life from God, not through our own devices. God reprimands us because He loves us and wants us to have a strong love for Him as well - none of this "lukewarm" business when it comes to a relationship with Him. We must repent of our lackluster faith in Him and work toward a deeper, more "in love" connection with our Heavenly Father, so that our relationship is like an exciting, magnetic need to be with God to which we just want to draw nearer and nearer to Him. Let's "light our faith fire," get excited about drawing closer to God and really work toward the kind of relationship God wants to have with each and every one of us.

Prayer

Dear Father in Heaven, help us all to "light our faith in You on fire," so that we feel drawn to you as a magnet - wanting to be closer and closer to you as our love for You grows beyond all measure, trying to match the love You have for us. Help us to not be afraid to share our faith in You with others and not to be ashamed of the love relationship we have with You. May we feel emboldened by our faith in You to further Your message here on earth, so that others might come to love You above all things as well. Amen.

Blessings of Fellowship

We declare to you what was from the beginning,
what we have heard, what we have seen with our eyes,
what we have looked at and touched with our hands,
concerning the word of life— this life was revealed,
and we have seen it and testify to it,
and declare to you the eternal life
that was with the Father and was revealed to us—
we declare to you what we have seen and heard
so that you also may have fellowship with us;
and truly our fellowship is with the Father
and with his Son Jesus Christ.
~ 1 John 1:1-3

Our church held a couple of festivals each year - one in June and one in September. They were meant not only to help raise funds toward our operating expenses, but also to be a time of food, fun and fellowship with each other and with those just visiting for the day. It was a great time to witness the love of Christ to those that are not a part of our faith family, yet are part of our community around us.

People have gathered together for centuries to celebrate different festivals for different reasons. Many were religious in nature and meant as a time of remembrance of historical events of the people celebrating them. Christians celebrate festivals to remember Christ's birth, death and resurrection. They also gather to fellowship together - supporting each other in Christian love during these celebrations.

Every day can be a time of fellowshipping with one another in the name of Christ Jesus. We do not have to wait for special events to do so. Being in fellowship with one another can be one-on-one as well as in large groups at church and in Bible studies - sharing our faith with one another to help strengthen each other's walk of faith through this earthly life we travel. Where can we find an opportunity to fellowship with someone today? You may make all the difference in the world to them. Then again, maybe they will be the very blessing from God you need today as well!

Prayer

Heavenly Father, we thank You for times to gather together to fellowship with one another - sharing our faith in You to help strengthen each other's walk through this earthly life. May we make a difference in each life we touch and may the lives that touch us also be a blessing to us from You. Amen.

Traveling Christ's Road

*See to it that no one takes you captive through philosophy
and empty deceit, according to human tradition,
according to the elemental spirits of the universe, and not
according to Christ. For in him the whole fullness of deity
dwells bodily, and you have come to fullness in him, who is
the head of every ruler and authority. In him also you were
circumcised with a spiritual circumcision,
by putting off the body of the flesh in the circumcision
of Christ; when you were buried with him in baptism,
you were also raised with him through faith
in the power of God, who raised him from the dead.
And when you were dead in trespasses
and the uncircumcision of your flesh, God made you alive
together with him, when he forgave us all our trespasses,
erasing the record that stood against us
with its legal demands. He set this aside,
nailing it to the cross.
He disarmed the rulers and authorities
and made a public example of them, triumphing
over them in it. Therefor do not let anyone condemn you
in matters of food and drink or of observing festivals,
new moons, or sabbaths. These are only a shadow
of what is to come, but the substance belongs to Christ.*
~ *Colossians 2:8-17*

Are you just like a vehicle on a muddy road? Stuck in a rut?
Feeling bogged down with life in general? This is when you
need to take a look around you and see where your focus lies.
Are you only traveling on the same old road that society has
had you on for far too long? A road that is a "short-cut" to
where you think you want to be?

Or is there another, less traveled road in much better condition that perhaps you should turn onto to continue your journey through life.

Christ has a far better road to travel on through this life to the next. We need to avoid the temptation of traveling the "short-cuts" that society tells us to take, for these roads tend to beat us up as we travel down them, leading us further and further from Christ. Instead, focus on traveling the "highway to heaven" in the direction of Christ. This doesn't mean there won't still be a pothole here and there that leaves us a bit jostled in our faith from time to time, but by following Christ's path that is outlined in His Word, we will have the tools necessary to keep ourselves together through this journey on earth. Christ has given us an "overhaul" through baptism - having cleaned all of the "gunk" that had built up in our lives - giving us a clean "engine" of a soul that runs by faith in Him. With Christ, we don't have to live by society's rules, for Christ's rules far outweigh the rules of society and will make us more like Him, which is another goal we wish to achieve in this journey. Society may ridicule us for taking Christ's road, but we know that His road is the safest and only way to get to where we truly want to be - in eternity with Him one day.

Prayer

Dearest Lord Jesus, life is a difficult road for us to travel. We have Your perfect example to follow, by reading, studying and meditating on Your Word and then following what You have told us to do. Even though we follow You, we know life still may not be easy here on earth, but we do know where we are heading when we obey Your direction. By following You, we have the peace of knowing that our destination of eternity with You is worth the journey we must take to get there. Thank You for Your guidance and mercy You give us at all times. Amen.

Harvest Time Palette

Very truly,
I tell you, unless a grain of wheat falls into the earth
and dies, it remains just a single grain;
but if it dies, it bears much fruit.
Those who love their life lose it,
and those who hate their life in this world
will keep it for eternal life.
~ John 12:24-25

Fall had arrived! The trees were beginning to turn their beautiful palette of colors, some of their leaves were drifting down softly on a breeze to the ground to cover the green grass with a layer of gold, red and brown. The fields were being harvested and the harvest dust hung heavily in the cool evening country air. The plants were giving up the fruits they have produced so that other life might carry on through the food they produced.

We, as Christians, must also "die" to ourselves to produce the "fruit" of the Spirit. Through this fruit, we provide the nourishment others need to grow in their faith and find the eternal life Christ offers us all. We must allow Christ to "harvest" our time to "feed" others through mission work and leading by example to show Christ's love. It is a "circle of life" to which we are called to be a part of. To not allow Christ to work through us would make us like a grain of wheat that remains a single grain - producing nothing and doing nothing to further others in their faith. To "die" by allowing ourselves, like grains of wheat, to be harvested, fall to the ground and become another plant, we can produce so much more than we can imagine for God's kingdom.

You must allow Christ to use you so that you can become so much more than you are by yourself. By doing this, you allow Christ's kingdom to grow through the nourishment of His love and Word through you. Are you ready to "die" to yourself in order to "live" a life that allows you to be so much more than you could imagine yourself to be? Allow Christ to harvest you and use you where He will. Become a beautiful part of His harvest palette!

Prayer

Christ in Heaven, thank You for allowing us to be "fruits of Your Spirit" to nourish others in their faith so that we can be a part of growing Your kingdom through our "dying" to ourselves by serving You. Amen.

PARENTAL SUPERVISION

Nevertheless I am continually with you;
you hold my right hand.
You guide me with your counsel,
and afterwards you will receive me with honor.
Whom have I in heaven but you?
And there is nothing on earth that I desire other than you.
My flesh and my heart may fail,
but God is the strength of my heart and my portion forever.
~ Psalm 73:23-26

Children require constant supervision. They tend to get into things they shouldn't when not being watched. When supervised, they tend to be more aware of what they can and cannot do. It is a learning process that spans many years. Hopefully, by being properly supervised, they will lean more toward what they should do as opposed to what they should not do when they mature into adulthood.

We, as Christians, are still children in God's eyes. He is always there to guide us in His ways. We want to please Him by doing what He calls us to do, although we may occasionally slip and "fall" away from His direction. God is strong enough to help "pick us back up" when we "fall" and put us back on His path. He is our Father that longs to have us walk into His arms for Him to embrace with His all-encompassing love.

Just as a child longs to be shown love and be protected, so we also long to feel the love of God enfolding us and keeping us from the evil around us in this world. We need to take the time to just sit in quiet meditation with God and allow Him to "hold" us in His love so that we can really "feel" that love strengthening us to carry out His will. Reading His Word is great and wonderful, but we need to allow time for His Word to "sink in" and really speak to us as a loving parent would speak to their child. In this way, we can better learn what it is God desires for us to do so that we can then go and carry out His will to please Him in response to the love we have for Him. By drawing closer to God and giving our lives over to Him, we gain a loving relationship with our Heavenly Father that will last for all eternity.

Prayer

Heavenly Father, take us by the hand and lead us where You wish us to go to fulfill whatever it is You desire us to do in Your Name. Give us the strength to carry out Your will so that You will be glorified. Thank you for Your love and desire for us to come closer to You. Amen.

Our Way or God's Way

'Jerusalem, Jerusalem, the city that kills the prophets
and stones those who are sent to it!
How often have I desired to gather your children together
as a hen gathers her brood under her wings,
and you were not willing!
~ Matthew 23:37

As children grow older, then tend to pull away from their parents and insert more and more independence. The parent longs to hold them and show them they are loved, but the children want nothing to do with it, often treating the parent as if they are embarrassed by them or being disrespectful to them. Not all children are this way, but it seems that in today's society, we see this more and more.

Things weren't any different in Jesus' day. The Jewish people had pulled away from God - making up their own rules to include with the laws given to them by God. They were no longer close to God. Instead, they wanted to do things their own way. They didn't listen to the signs of the time - recorded throughout their Holy Word. Had they paid attention, they may have seen the ultimate sign of God's love standing right among them. Instead, they scorned Jesus. They later punished Him and put Him to death. God had the ultimate gift of love right in front of their eyes and allowed His own son to die for the sins of all people so that they could one day come back to Him and join Him in His Heavenly kingdom.

God longs to gather us all to Him in His loving embrace. We are His children that He paid so high a price for. Are we willing to be gathered to Him? Are we willing to put away our stubbornness and allow God to fill us with His love? Or are we going to continue to pull away from Him to "do our own thing? The choice is ours to make. Just remember, we only have "forever" by choosing God and His love for us, and "forever" doesn't wait.

Prayer

Heavenly Father, thank You for Your unconditional love for us, despite our selfish ways. Help us to choose wisely by choosing to let You take control of our lives and fill us with Your perfect love for all eternity. Amen.

ABUNDANT HARVEST GIFTS

Do not be deceived; God is not mocked,
for you reap whatever you sow.
If you sow to your own flesh,
you will reap corruption from the flesh;
but if you sow to the Spirit,
you will reap eternal life from the Spirit.
So let us not grow weary in doing what is right,
for we will reap at harvest time, if we do not give up.
So then, whenever we have an opportunity,
let us work for the good of all,
and especially for those of the family of faith.
*~ **Galatians 6:7-10***

Harvest time was here! The bounty had been very plentiful, with excesses being deposited in our church parking lot by a generous farmer for distribution by church members to area food pantries. Many who had little were being blessed by the generosity of a farmer who had been blessed by God with an abundant harvest. Without giving of the abundance to those in need, the excess produce would just rot in the fields.

Everyone can be a blessing to others if they allow themselves to be "harvested" by God of His Spiritual fruits within each one of them. The many talents each person has can be used to further the kingdom of God and bless those less fortunate if they allow God to use them as He wishes. By not allowing their "fruits" to be harvested by God, they are like the vines that are ignored in the field and the produce rots on the vine in the field, giving off a foul odor to all who go near that field.

154

You can only benefit this world by allowing God to work within you, lest you sit idly by and "rot" in your field. Are you ready to be harvested by God? Allow God to use you to bless His kingdom here on earth now. He will reward you in heaven later.

Prayer

Dear Lord, harvest me and use my talents You have blessed me with to help others in Your name. Do not allow me to sit idly by and rot - letting these precious talents go to waste. Amen.

GIVE TO THE LEAST ~ INHERIT THE KINGDOM

Then the king will say to those at his right hand,
"Come, you that are blessed by my Father,
inherit the kingdom prepared for you
from the foundation of the world;
for I was hungry and you gave me food,
I was thirsty and you gave me something to drink,
I was a stranger and you welcomed me,
I was naked and you gave me clothing,
I was sick and you took care of me,
I was in prison and you visited me."
Then the righteous will answer him,
"Lord, when was it that we saw you hungry
and gave you food,
or thirsty and gave you something to drink?
And when was it that we saw you a stranger
and welcomed you,
or naked and gave you clothing?
And when was it that we saw you sick
or in prison and visited you?"
And the king will answer them,
"Truly I tell you, just as you did it to one of the least of these
who are members of my family, you did it to me."
*~ **Matthew 25:34-40***

Parents help their children, not only when they are growing up, but even during adulthood. This is just the nature of things. Parents do not like to see their children struggling - especially when they need something that will keep them safe or will further their career, but the child may not not have the funds with which to handle such expenses at that particular moment. Parents try to step in and help their children when needed, even after they have grown up - at least they try when the grown child allows them to help.

God is like this as well. He does not like to see His children struggling with hunger, joblessness, homelessness, addictions, loneliness, pain and illness. He tries to step in where and when His children allow Him to intervene on their behalf, but sometimes, it takes more than just God's own divine intervention. Sometimes, it takes His other children to be His instruments of His peace to intervene in His name. God expects us, as His children, to care for one another. When we see others in need, we are to share His love by reaching out to those less fortunate and help care for them.

This is what we were created for - to be reflections of God's love to each other, as well as to love God. The way to best love God is to share His love with others. Isn't it time we do this very thing? There are many ways in which we can share God's love with others less fortunate within our own communities as well as around the world. We need to find our way to share God's love every day and take action.

Prayer

Dear Lord, help us to be more aware of the needs of others around us and to share Your love with them in whatever way they need help, not just notice them and walk away. Amen.

157

SHARING IS CARING

We know love by this, that he laid down his life for us
—and we ought to lay down our lives for one another.
How does God's love abide in anyone
who has the world's goods and sees a brother or sister in
need and yet refuses help?
~ 1 John 3:16-17

We, as Christians, have a calling from God to serve others out of the love we have for our Heavenly Father. We do this in response to the love of God within us. This love must be shared with others - especially those in need. If we do not share this love from our Father, what good is it? It is like a beautiful fruit that we look at and admire, yet if we do not partake of this fruit, it will rot and go to waste - not fulfilling its purpose on earth by being nourishment for our body. So is the love of God within each of us. We must share it with others to nourish our souls by sharing God's love with others.

When we see others in this world that are in need, we must show them the love of God. By sharing our love from God, we help bring life to those in need. Hoarding our earthly items and putting them above sharing God's love is a slap in the face to God. He provides what we have to be shared in His name.

If you cannot share what God has given you, why should God continue to bless you? He gave His only Son to die for all that you do wrong so that you might live through His ultimate sacrifice! How much are you willing to sacrifice to show God how much you love Him?

Prayer

Heavenly Father, help us to love You above all else and to show Your love to others in need. Thank you for the many blessings You have given us so that we can share those blessings with others in Your name. Amen.

Heavenly Hand-Made Gifts

May the glory of the Lord endure for ever;
may the Lord rejoice in his works—
who looks on the earth and it trembles,
who touches the mountains and they smoke.
I will sing to the Lord as long as I live;
I will sing praise to my God while I have being.
May my meditation be pleasing to him,
for I rejoice in the Lord.
*~ **Psalm 104:31-34***

We had been enjoying beautiful, fall weather one mid-October. My co-worker loved the outdoors and had expanded my horizons by getting me away from my desk to eat lunch at the picnic table on our beautiful church grounds that once was home to annual Campground revival meetings. The light breeze wafted golden leaves from their branches into the air and gently glided them to the ground, twisting and turning the rays of sunlight. It made for a beautiful scene. As my co-worker put it, it looked like a "leaf globe", instead of a snow globe! The golden shimmers made for an entrancing scene on this beautiful day.

It is good to take time out of our busy schedules and just sit and marvel at God's handiwork. We so often rush about, ignoring the scenery God created for us to enjoy! We should take time every day to enjoy all that God has created for us and to praise Him for all he has done for us. What a wonderfully awesome Father He is!

Prayer

Heavenly Father, thank You for all of the beauty You have created for us to enjoy and for all that You give us daily. May we always praise You for all of the wonderful works of Your hand! Amen.

Oh, What a Relief It Is!

By the tender mercy of our God,
the dawn from on high will break upon us,
to give light to those who sit in darkness
and in the shadow of death,
to guide our feet into the way of peace.'
~ Luke 1:78-79

Peace is a word that comes up so often in the Bible. Both the Old and New Testaments refer to it often, like a cherished treasure that is sought after, as well as a gift from God. This gift is something we all look for in our lives, but there is only one way to find it.

God blessed us with His presence through His only Son to come show us the way to peace in our lives. By following Christ's example of living our lives in service to God, we can truly find the peace within our souls that we so long for. This peace fills us as we serve God and is such a wonderful feeling to be free of fear and worry so that we can live our lives knowing that all is well when we rest in God's hands.

God will take care of His children, just as we care for our own children. Oh, what a relief it is to know that God is there to protect us, guide us and provide for us when we follow and serve Him. He is all we need for true peace in our lives.

Prayer

Dear Lord, thank You for the peace that only You can give us through Your Son, Jesus Christ. Amen.

GIVING IN FAITH

He looked up and saw rich people
putting their gifts into the treasury;
he also saw a poor widow put in two small copper coins.
He said, 'Truly I tell you,
this poor widow has put in more than all of them;
for all of them have contributed out of their abundance,
but she out of her poverty has put in all she had to live on.'
*~ **Luke 24:1-4***

In 2006, I went to a PAUMCS (Professional Administrators of the United Methodist Connectional Structure) Convention in Pasadena, California. Between meetings, they had items for sale, one of which was a necklace with a coin that had been found at a dig near the old Temple of Jerusalem. It is said that it was a widow's mite - worth very little in its day - even less than a penny is to us today.

In Jesus' time, He spoke of the temple treasury, where many wealthy people would make a production of how much they were giving as an offering to God. In comparison, this poor widow quietly drops in two small coins - widow's mites - that were a mere pittance compared to the offerings of the others. How could her two small coins be more than the amount of the other offerings?

If you compared it to the percentage of what each person was giving at the time, those making a large production of their offerings and how much they were giving were giving a mere pittance in the percentage of what they had - giving from their excess and not greatly affecting how they would be able to support themselves on what they kept. This poor widow gave

ALL she had - 100% - as an offering to God, knowing that God would provide for her, even though she now had nothing left to give. Her faith in God and His provision for her was far greater than that of the more wealthy givers. Those giving from their excess didn't trust God to take care of them. Instead, those that were more financially well off trusted in themselves and what they were able to provide to take care of them instead of trusting in God.

Where do you put your faith? In yourself and what you can provide? Or do you put your faith in God and what He can give you? The decision is yours to make.

Prayer

Heavenly Father, You provide all that we have. Help us to remember that when we gift back to You from that which You have provided to us. Let us always put our faith in You and not ourselves to see that we have all that we need. Amen.

COMMUNICATE BOLDLY

Thus I make it my ambition to proclaim the good news,
not where Christ has already been named,
so that I do not build on someone else's foundation,
but as it is written,
'Those who have never been told of him shall see,
and those who have never heard of him shall understand.'
~ ***Romans 15:20-21***

Paul wrote boldly to the church in Rome as to what his mission in life was. His mission was as it still should be for the churches around the world - to take the message of Christ to those who have still not heard of His saving grace. With communication as it is today compared to in the days of the early Christian church, it is hard to believe that there are still people who have never heard about Christ, but they do still exist.

This weekend, we will host our missionary from Cookson Hills Mission in Oklahoma. Meri Whitaker will be telling our congregation about her work with the Native Americans on the reservation that she serves and that we help to support, not only in contributing to her salary, but also with contributions to this community of people that have so little and to which we send members to work on mission trips during the year.

Through our contributions, work, service, prayers and financial support, we hope to further the message of Christ and His grace to this community of people that are less fortunate financially than we are here. May our gifts and service help to show Christ's love to them and lead them to a relationship with Christ. Let us remember that we are here to serve God as His messengers of the Good News and further His kingdom while we are here on earth so that all who live might know of Christ and be saved through Him.

Prayer

Father in Heaven, thank you for missionaries that give up their lives in service to You so that others may be led to You and Your Son's saving grace. May we do all in our power to support these missionaries in their work. Use us as You will, Lord. Amen.

Refuge of Joy and Peace

He left that place and came to his home town,
and his disciples followed him.
On the sabbath he began to teach in the synagogue,
and many who heard him were astounded.
They said, 'Where did this man get all this?
What is this wisdom that has been given to him?
What deeds of power are being done by his hands!
Is not this the carpenter, the son of Mary
and brother of James and Joses and Judas and Simon,
and are not his sisters here with us?'
And they took offence at him.
Then Jesus said to them, 'Prophets are not without honor,
except in their home town,
and among their own kin, and in their own house.'
And he could do no deed of power there,
except that he laid his hands on a few sick people
and cured them.
And he was amazed at their unbelief.
*~ **Mark 5:1-6***

Many of us find it easier to smile at strangers and remain even-tempered, even in difficult conversations with people we do not know well. We have also heard stories of parents who talk about their children getting rave reviews by teachers and others outside of the family, and these parents seem surprised and asked if they were talking about the same children! When we are at home, however, we tend to let our guard down and show our true feelings and emotions to those around us. They see us as we are as a whole - the good, the bad and the ugly.

Jesus found the same problem in His time. People raved about

His miracles and teachings outside of the town He grew up in, but the people that had watched Him grow up found it harder to believe that Jesus could be the Messiah. To them, Jesus was an ordinary man! How could He be so special?

We need to be aware that even our own family members need to be treated with the respect and politeness that we so freely give to others outside of the family. We may take them for granted and not always see how special they are, but we all are very unique and special in God's eyes. It is time we step back and re-evaluate how we behave in public vs. how we behave at home and make a conscious effort to be on our best behavior to everyone at all times. In this way, our homes will always be a refuge of joy and peace instead of allowing negative feelings and behavior cloud our doorways.

Prayer

Dear Jesus, it is so hard to be on our best behavior in public and not to let our guard down once we step through the threshold of our own homes - allowing pent up feelings and emotions take their toll on our closest loved ones. Help us to always look for the positives in life - even at home - so that our lives reflect Your love to all around us at all times. Please, keep the negative thoughts and feelings from taking hold of us in our homes so that our homes are always a refuge of joy and peace. Amen.

BE THANKFUL IN EVERYTHING

But we appeal to you, brothers and sisters,
to respect those who labor among you,
and have charge of you in the Lord and admonish you;
esteem them very highly in love because of their work.
Be at peace among yourselves. XAnd we urge you,
beloved, to admonish the idlers, encourage the faint-hearted,
help the weak, be patient with all of them.
See that none of you repays evil for evil,
but always seek to do good to one another and to all.
Rejoice always, pray without ceasing,
give thanks in all circumstances;
for this is the will of God in Christ Jesus for you.
Do not quench the Spirit.
Do not despise the words of prophets,
but test everything; hold fast to what is good;
abstain from every form of evil.

May the God of peace himself sanctify you entirely;
and may your spirit and soul and body be kept sound and
blameless at the coming of our Lord Jesus Christ.
~ 1 Thessalonians 5:12-23

Sunday started out as a cloudy fall day, just a couple of weeks away from Thanksgiving. We had just held a special offering for people affected by the terrible typhoon in the Philippines. Little did we know that disaster was just around the corner in our own area of the country. Just a couple of hours away, while many of the small towns' population was attending church, their homes and all that they owned were blown away in an instant by tornadoes that touched down throughout Central Illinois.

How can people be thankful in situations such as these? For one, God knew His people would be honoring Him through worship, so the death and injury count of such storms was very low. God did not punish those who love Him, but instead, kept them safe in His own house. These same churches have now become shelters for those that are not able to return to their homes.

Secondly, the country has rallied together to care for those that have lost so much in these terrible storms. Donations are coming from all over, as well as many volunteers traveling to help clean up the area so that the victims can begin their rebuilding process.

Finally, debris has been found almost 100 miles from the areas hit by the storms. Photographs, documents, etc. are being gathered together to be returned to the areas to be reclaimed by the victims. Thanks to today's communication abilities through things like Facebook, some of these items were recognized and arrangements made to be returned to the owner the same day! The return of these items might seem minor to those that have gathered them from their yards, but to those that lost so much, it is just one more item that they still have or will receive back soon after having lost so much.

What difficulties are you faced with? Even in difficult times, you can find things to be thankful for and must remember to praise God for His many blessings and mercies. God is so very good!

Prayer

Heavenly Father, we thank you for keeping so many of Your children safe during the terrible storms, even while their lives outside of your protection were being blown away. Help us all to remember the many blessings and mercies You give all of us each day, despite the many turmoils going on in our lives and the lives around us. Amen.

THANK GOD

And let the peace of Christ rule in your hearts,
to which indeed you were called in the one body.
And be thankful.
*~ **Colossians 3:15***

There are often times that families are in discord and not speaking to one another. It is a sad situation, no matter what the reason. Sometimes they reunite just before a loved one passes. Other times, regret occurs because the loved ones never reconcile before one of them passes away.

I had a couple of cousins - sisters - that didn't speak for several years. They were still not even able to be in the same room with one another when it came time to celebrate their mother's 80th birthday. Just two weeks before the mother passed away at the age of 83, they finally reconciled. I'm sure it put their mother at ease after all of these years to finally have her family reunited once again and for peace to come back into her family life.

How often do we find ourselves feuding over silly things? How often do we pull away from family and friends because it seems too difficult for us to swallow our pride to bury the hatchet? How many of us have been estranged from others and don't even remember the original reason the spat occurred in the first place?

God wants us to fill our hearts and minds with the peace of Christ and to be thankful for all that we have. This includes being thankful and making peace with all those that are in our lives for one reason or another. Life is too short to waste on silly, trivial spats that take valuable time away from relationships. Let us all strive this Thanksgiving to make amends with all those we are in discord with and truly thank the Lord for the many blessings each person is to us in our lives.

Prayer

Heavenly Father, let us always be reminded to never let things come between us and those we love. Help us to always strive to make amends so that we don't waste the time we have with each person in our lives by fighting, not speaking to one another, or holding grudges. Help us to always keep our hearts and minds filled with Christ's peace and be thankful for all You have given us. Amen.

FINDING HOPE IN SILENCE

For God alone my soul waits in silence,
for my hope is from him.
~ Psalm 62:5

The season of preparation for the celebration of the birth of Christ was upon us. The decorations were being dragged out of storage and placed in the places they grace in the home each year. The lights were going on inside and out to light the way to the newborn king.

Some, however, find that they dread the season's arrival. Loved ones have gone on ahead, leaving an empty place in hearts and homes. Illness may have stricken families and have taken much of the joy out of their lives as they worry about the outcome of their treatments. The season will bring upon these very people a great sadness as they find it difficult to carry on celebrations that have been such a part of their lives for so many years.

One might ask how others can be so happy when their own lives are so filled with pain and sorrow. That is when one must remember that God is always there, even in the midst of the sorrow and pain of life. This is the very reason He came to earth in the form of a newborn babe. He wanted to experience life from the human perspective. This included all of the love, joy, happiness, illness, sadness, pain and loss. He fully understands what humans are going through on a daily basis and wants to comfort those who are hurting as well as celebrate with those experiencing the joys of life.

Let us all remember that, no matter what is happening in our lives, good or bad, God is there with us to experience whatever life throws our way. Our souls may always find comfort and peace when we sit and wait for God in the silence of our lives to give us the hope we need to carry on. We are never alone.

Prayer

Lord, we thank You for the great love You have for all of us, that You were willing to come to earth in the form of a human infant to experience life as we all live and see it. Only You can fully understand our inner thoughts and can comfort us and strengthen us as we need and when we need it most. We silently wait for You in the hope that all will be well with our souls today and in the future when we seek Your presence with us. Amen.

LETTING GO AND LETTING GOD

He heals the broken-hearted,
and binds up their wounds.
~ Psalm 147:3

Once again, in the cold of the morning, I wandered back to the coffee machine and looked out the window as my hot cup of "comfort" poured out for me. Looking across the once lush ravine, I saw the remnants of the spring storms in the form of broken and uprooted trees that had been hidden from view by the green leaves of spring and summer. Now that fall has stripped the covering away, the damage can be seen as it truly is.

Many people are hurt and broken-hearted, but put on a good facade when in the company of others. They do not wish for anyone to know their true feelings, they may think that these feelings make them feel inferior to others around them, or they just do not want to make others feel saddened by their plight. God, however, can see all things. He sees through the show of "all is well" and wants to ease the pain and broken spirit within all of us.

In our times of sadness and pain, we need to remember to turn to God and leave all our troubles and burdens for Him to carry so that we can regain the joy and happiness He so much wants us to have in our lives. This healing is not always instantaneous, but a healing process does begin when we give over all of our unwanted feelings of hurt, loss and worry to God. His shoulders are much larger than ours and can carry the load we no longer want to have to deal with alone.

As this Holy Season approaches, let us remember to hand all of our unwanted burdens over to God and allow His gift of Christ light the way to happier, more joy-filled days ahead. Always remember that He gave us His only Son as the ultimate gift of His love for us and it is with this love that He desires to have a close, intimate relationship with each of us. He will always take care of us. We just have to let go of trying to handle everything ourselves and let God "take the wheel."

Prayer

Father in Heaven, I no longer want to have to deal with the undesirable feelings of worry, pain, and loss. Please, take these burdens from me and lead me to the joy, peace and happiness that you want me to have in my life. Help me to lead others to You in this same way, so that they can experience life as You have always wanted them to live it. In Christ's name I pray. Amen.

SPREADING THE WORD

And he said to them,
'Go into all the world and proclaim the good news
to the whole creation.
*~ **Mark 16:15***

As I was going through my e-mails, I stumbled across one that, at first, I thought was a spam message that had infiltrated through my virus program and settled in my in box. As I looked to delete it, something drew me back to the message. It was from a new pastor in South Africa, requesting old Bibles of any types, any religious works written by men of God, and study materials that might further his ministry in Africa.

My initial reaction to delete the message was slowed at this point as I further scanned this message for any link that may have been placed into the message to "click" on and send a virus through my computer. There was none. I began to think that this young pastor may have gotten my e-mail through a book I had ordered a few months ago from South Africa, written by Retha and Aldo McPherson about Aldo's experience in heaven after a terrible accident. This may be a completely "on the level" request from a young pastor desperate to begin his new ministry with as much religious materials as he can lay his hands on.

I am by no means telling people to open e-mails from people they do not know, but I am saying to be careful not to write off all random e-mails as virus carriers. There are occasions that these e-mails are messages sent by people of God looking for help from around the world to advance God's word in their part of the world that we cannot reach ourselves. God may be opening a door here for us to look at what we have and no longer use to be used anew in another area of the world to advance His kingdom.

What resources have you used and no longer use as study materials to grow closer to God? Where can they be used again to remain useful to others? It may be time to "clean house" and put those religious materials to good use where they are needed most.

Prayer

Heavenly Father, we thank you for the many resources You have provided to us to learn more about You and to grow stronger in our faith in You. May we share these resources with others when they have outgrown their usefulness to us so that others may experience You in their growing faith as well. Amen.

LEARNING TO WAIT

For the grace of God has appeared,
bringing salvation to all,
training us to renounce impiety and worldly passions,
and in the present age to live lives that are self-controlled,
upright, and godly,
while we wait for the blessed hope and the manifestation
of the glory of our great God and Savior, Jesus Christ.
*~ **Titus 2:11-13***

The drive to work one morning was a bit frustrating for me, as I am one of the "offensive" drivers all other drivers are to drive "defensively" for. I get frustrated when people who are too afraid to drive correctly for the weather creep along at a "turtle pace," creating more of a road hazard than the weather conditions themselves. I often find myself wanting to "nudge" them along and often hear myself telling them to either drive right or stay off of the road (not that they can hear me with my windows up against the cold, snowy conditions). Yet, as I accelerate around a corner in the poorly-plowed roads and feel the back end of the vehicle wanting to slide a bit, I let off of the accelerator to make sure that I do not lose control and realize that perhaps the conditions are not as good as I think they may be and that those slower drivers may have better sense than I do.

We must, as Christians, train ourselves to go against the worldly passions and live our lives more in line with the self-control, uprightness and godliness that the Lord has requested we live our lives like. When we do this, we are better able to wait for the blessings and glory of God in our lives that have been promised to us. This is very hard to do in today's fast-paced world, but it is possible to do if we really put our minds to it. It just takes a lot of determination to learn to wait on God's timing in our lives instead of pushing ahead on our own for a faster outcome of what we would like to see happen.

Prayer

Heavenly Father, thank you for all You have given us and promise to give to those who are faithful to You. Help us to learn to wait on Your timing and not try to force our own timetables on what we want when we want it. Amen.

THE MORE YOU GIVE, THE MORE YOU RECEIVE

He who supplies seed to the sower
and bread for food will supply
and multiply your seed for sowing
and increase the harvest of your righteousness.
You will be enriched in every way for your great generosity,
which will produce thanksgiving to God through us;
for the rendering of this ministry
not only supplies the needs of the saints
but also overflows with many thanksgivings to God.
Through the testing of this ministry you glorify God
by your obedience to the confession of the gospel of Christ
and by the generosity of your sharing with them
and with all others,
while they long for you and pray for you
because of the surpassing grace of God
that he has given you.
Thanks be to God for his indescribable gift!
*~ **2 Corinthians 9:10-15***

It never ceases to amaze me when I see the generosity of others after hearing of an extreme need somewhere by someone. Be it a request from a nearby community after a weather disaster, a global mission's cry for help half way around the world, or even one of their own in their community during difficult times, the outpouring of love and care from others can bring one to tears. Not only are the recipients blessed by the giving, but so are those that have done the giving. There is no way to really describe the feeling one gets when they see the reaction of those whose needs are filled. It fills one with an overwhelming joy that they were able to help in some small way to brighten the life of someone else, but even this seems to be a lame description for the actual feelings experienced by the giver.

God saw His creation falling away from Him generation after generation, with only a faithful few keeping the faith alive. He finally gave the ultimate gift of His one and only Son to redeem us to Him. The pain God had to endure as He watched His Son die on the cross alone had to be excruciating, yet the joy that has come from this selfless act of love has been multiplied exponentially! Not only did His Son remain faithful - even through death - but so many of God's children have been reconciled to Him through Jesus' ultimate sacrifice! Love isn't love until it is given away, which is what God has done and continues to offer us every day.

Are you ready to give in order to receive? It isn't difficult. Let God's Holy Spirit guide you and you will feel the amazing joy and love return to you multiplied many times over as you continue to give in His name.

Prayer

Heavenly Father, guide me in the way you wish me to share Your love with others so that the blessings You have given me may be multiplied many times over. Thank you for the love and joy I experience as I do Your will in all things, as they bless me more than I can relate in words. Amen.

Harmony Vs. Haughty

Live in harmony with one another; do not be haughty,
but associate with the lowly;
do not claim to be wiser than you are.
~ Romans 12:16

My husband and I just had just finished a stay at a beautiful resort for our anniversary. While there, we noticed all of the "beautiful people" staying there - many expecting to be waited on hand and foot by the staff and leaving behind messes that most polite people would take care of themselves. I understand that when staying at these places, that you pay for people to wait on you, but there is still what I consider common courtesy by those being waited on to those that serve them that still should be maintained.

My husband and I always made sure to pick up as much of our room as we could before housekeeping came in to service the room. We greeted all of the staff we saw if they didn't beat us to the greeting first. We never were demanding of the staff and always thanked them for whatever service they were providing. We even saw one of the staff at the mall on their day off and that particular staff person made sure to greet us and make light conversation in passing. This same staff member greeted us again the next morning at breakfast just before we left the resort to go home. He made sure he took my plate from me and insisted that he carry it to my table and spoke with us again briefly. It was a sad farewell for us, as this was definitely an "Eden" place for our vacation stay. My husband then surprised a couple of other staff members who were struggling with a couple of tasks. I don't think they were used to having someone staying there stopping to help them.

They thanked my husband heartily with very large smiles and words of appreciation as we continued our final walk on the beach and around the pool.

As I stop to think about this while I waited for a flight back to the cold and snow of Chicago, I realized that the more we offer smiles, greetings and aid to others, the more we get in return - especially when those we are helping are so often taken for granted by others. By noticing them and letting them feel equal and appreciated, you may make their entire day! There are many times those with jobs that are taken for granted may feel under-appreciated and devalued by what they have to do for a living compared to those they are serving, yet there is a place for everyone and all jobs need to be done, therefore, they should be considered equal in the body of Christ and appreciated just as much as someone with some job that is considered important and high- paying.

Who do you see around you every day that you take for granted? Have you thanked them for the good job they are doing? Will you make their day brighter by acknowledging them on equal ground? Will you stoop to help them where you can to lighten their load?

Prayer

Heavenly Father, we thank you for all those that have taken on the jobs we have no desire to do ourselves that make our lives easier. Help us to always acknowledge them and lend a hand when we can to brighten their day as they serve others. Amen.

TREASURE HUNTING

I want their hearts to be encouraged and united in love,
so that they may have all the riches of assured understanding
and have the knowledge of God's mystery,
that is, Christ himself, in whom are hidden all the treasures
of wisdom and knowledge.
*~ **Colossians 2:2-3***

I know I often speak of looking out the window in the morning while getting my coffee before heading to my desk to really "get down to work." It is so inspiring to see nature in the morning - especially when God's other creatures are doing the inspiring. I noticed 8 squirrels running around in the snow - two were each chasing another squirrel, and the other four were running short "jaunts" here and there in different directions, pausing to dig for something and quickly rose to eat whatever it was that they had found buried in the snow. They remind me of a pirate in a movie, following a treasure map and taking exaggerated strides - first one way, then another - to locate the desired treasure at the "X" on the map.

We have just such a map in the form of a book - the Holy Bible - that leads us to the treasure that our souls are all yearning for. Reading it carefully and following its direction helps lead us to this treasure of life that springs eternal for our souls in heaven. Earthly treasurers tend to not bring us the satisfaction and fulfillment that we sometimes think they will, but a relationship with God through Christ will fill our souls to overflowing - nourishing us with His love and mercy so that we can become heirs adopted into heaven as God's own children. There is no greater treasure than this!

Prayer

Heavenly Father, thank you for your treasure given to us in the form of Your Son, who reconciles us to You so that we can be called Your children. Help us to make time to seek Your truth through Your Word daily, so that we can continue to grow closer to You. Amen.

Not Always as It Seems

When God saw what they did,
how they turned from their evil ways,
God changed his mind about the calamity
that he had said he would bring upon them;
and he did not do it.

But this was very displeasing to Jonah,
and he became angry.
He prayed to the Lord and said, 'O Lord!
Is not this what I said while I was still in my own country?
That is why I fled to Tarshish at the beginning;
for I knew that you are a gracious God and merciful,
slow to anger, and abounding in steadfast love,
and ready to relent from punishing.
And now, O Lord, please take my life from me,
for it is better for me to die than to live.'
and the Lord said, 'Is it right for you to be angry?'

And should I not be concerned about Nineveh,
that great city, in which there are more than
a hundred and twenty thousand people
who do not know their right hand from their left,
and also many animals?'
*~ **Jonah 3:10, 4:1-4, 11***

Centuries ago, Jonah was sure that he was delivering a pronouncement of coming judgment on Nineveh, but God chose, instead, to grant mercy to this city that had listened to the message delivered by Jonah and repented of their sinfulness and turned back to worshiping God. This greatly upset Jonah, who found it difficult to accept that the message

186

he delivered was not fulfilled by God. He didn't understand why God had changed His mind. The purpose of the message from God was not so much to punish, as it was to get people to recognize their sinful ways, repent and return to God.

I have often been told that I have a tone to my voice that I don't realize I have. Even as a child growing up and speaking to my parents, I would have "that tone" that they took as "back-talk," when I didn't feel I was speaking disrespectfully at the time. Even today, my spouse or children will tell me I have "that tone" or I will accuse my spouse of the very same thing - interpreting a meaning with the tone I am hearing that was not intended to be relayed to me in the first place. This can cause arguments very easily when I tend to "read into" words and actions more than there was meant to be.

We need to always be mindful that how we interpret what we hear, (as well as how we relay our own messages to others). Taking what we hear with a grain of salt and letting the "possible hurt feelings" just run off of our backs like "water off a duck's bill" is sometimes the best way to handle conversations that upset us. It doesn't mean that we shouldn't look for the message we are to be receiving, but instead look for how this message is to help us in the future - not taking it too much to heart, allowing it to hurt us when that was never the intention of the message in the first place. Hurt feelings do not help us better ourselves, but messages meant to help our decision making in the future IS good for us. We all need to try to always separate the message from the feelings when the message might initially sound hurtful - it may not be meant to hurt us at all - and quickly forgive anything that might lead us to believe anything other than to that it is to help us in the long run.

Prayer

Lord, help us to always listen for the real messages being given to us by others instead of misinterpreting their messages from a tone of voice or allowing it to hurt us in a way that it was never meant to. Help us to always find what a message is trying to teach us and use it to grow in ways that better ourselves and our lives with one another. Let us not hold onto hurt feelings, but rather forgive those that may have had no intention of hurting us in the first place, for they only have our best interests at heart, as do You. Amen.

FOLLOWING THE RULES

Obey your leaders and submit to them, for they are keeping
watch over your souls and will give an account.
Let them do this with joy and not with sighing—
for that would be harmful to you.
~ Hebrews 13:17

How often do we think that rules and laws pertain to others, but not ourselves? How often do we feel that we are invincible? We often see others bending or breaking the rules and think to ourselves how crazy the offenders are, but do we ever view ourselves in that way when we bend or break the rules to suit ourselves?

My husband and I drove through the Smoky Mountain National Forest. We love to visit Cades Cove and view any wildlife that meander through the area on our scenic drive. We especially enjoy when that wildlife happens to be a bear, for we don't see them up in "our neck of the woods" in northern Illinois.

I was starting to feel a little disappointed that we hadn't seen any bear in our two days of driving through the Cove. We continued our scenic tour along the winding road between the Cove and Gatlinburg, when we saw many cars pulled off to the side of the road, a female ranger quickly walking toward a group of people all looking up the hill and then spotted almost a half dozen men that had crossed the stream and were standing in different areas up the hill, pointing cameras and camera phones further up the hill. The ranger was yelling for them to get back to the road. Looking farther up the hill, we could see a mama bear slowly walking up the hill, turning to keep an eye on her cub that was slowly following her at a distance.

My first reaction was, "oh, how cute! I have finally seen a bear on this trip!" Then I realized that the men trying to get closer pictures of the animals really were not being very smart. This was not a petting zoo! The mama bear was not a docile creature, as she appeared in her slow, laid-back style of walk. She could have turned at any moment and severely harmed or killed one of these men if she felt that her cub was in danger. The ranger was doing her job to keep the "not so bright" men from continuing their quest by calling them back before the mama bear became threatened. She was also keeping the mama bear safe, for if the mama attacked, the mama would have to be put down, leaving her cub orphaned.

Rules and laws are made for reasons that we may or may not always agree with, but they serve a purpose. Not following them may create harm not only for us, but for others involved as well - be "the other" a fellow human or other creature of nature. Thinking that we are exceptions to the rules creates more problems for those trying to enforce them. By not obeying and becoming harmed in the process, the person or persons enforcing these rules and laws may suffer consequences that they do not deserve to be punished for. They may be harmed in the process of protecting the offenders, or they may be reprimanded by their superiors for situations that they were not able to fully control.

When we are "out and about," we need to remember that God has placed people, rules and laws here to help protect us. We need to consciously follow these rules and listen to those in authority so that, not only are we kept safe, but so are those around us. We are not omnipotent, even though we like to think that trouble will only come to other offenders. Following the rules will keep us safe to enjoy another beautiful God-given day.

Prayer

Dear Lord, thank You for the rules, laws and people You have placed here to enforce them. Thank You for keeping our best interests at heart and help us to listen to and follow these rules so that we, and others, remain safe as we enjoy the lives You have blessed us with. Amen.

SECRET ACTS

*They show that what the law requires
is written on their hearts,
to which their own conscience also bears witness;
and their conflicting thoughts will accuse
or perhaps excuse them on the day when,
according to my gospel, God, through Jesus Christ,
will judge the secret thoughts of all.*
~ ***Romans 2:15-16***

We had been the recipients of a secret act twice in 48 hours. This act was a wonderful surprise, as it was the gift of secretly plowing our driveway while we were gone. Each time, my husband had full intentions of getting out the snow blower as soon as we got home, only to be greeted with the job already done! It allowed him more relaxation time - something he has very little of during this time of year.

People throughout the ages have often done things in secret. Some were for good, but others were not. Things done in secret are never hidden from God's eyes. These "secret acts" show what is really in the hearts of those doing them. Often, what people do in public is to give an impression of how people want to be perceived, when in reality, what they do in secret is who they really are as a person. This "secret" identity will be judged one day - either condemning the person or redeeming them in the eyes of God. Nothing done - publicly or in secret - is missed by God and all will be judged for all they do.

What do you do for others to see? What do you do secretly that you don't want others to know about? Remember, everything you do - known or unknown to others - will determine your eternal reward someday. Act wisely in all you do at all times.

Prayer

Lord, thank You for always seeing us for who we really are. Knowing this, we must always remember that the eternal judgment awaits us all and that we must always seek to do what is right in Your eyes - both in public and in secret. Amen.

Appreciation of Beauty

One thing I asked of the Lord,
that will I seek after:
to live in the house of the Lord
all the days of my life,
to behold the beauty of the Lord,
and to inquire in his temple.
*~ **Psalm 27:4***

What a glorious day it was! The sun was shining, the sky was clear and the new blanket of snow coated everything in a beautiful white blanket. Yes, it was bitterly cold out, but when one are looked out on the beautiful day through the window of a warm building, it was still enjoyable to behold.

As I gazed out this beautiful scene, a bright red cardinal perched momentarily on the "church" bird feeder outside of my kitchen window. The contrast between the white of the snow and the red of his feathers was breathtaking. It is moments like this that I pause and think of just how great God's creation is - how majestic His masterpieces are all around us!

As we walk throughout our day today - and everyday – we need to take a moment and just look for what amazing thing we may take for granted most of the time and ponder at just how wonderful God has created it - and all things - so that we can enjoy life and it's many treasures while we are here on this earth. They are the many gifts of love that He has blessed us with that are just a foretaste of the beauty that awaits us one day when we join Him in His glorious kingdom, for which there is no match for the beauty within. We then need to thank Him for all that He has given for us to enjoy in this life while we await His call for us to "come home" to His glory one day.

Prayer

Lord, we thank you for the many beautiful gifts You have blessed us with each and every day to enjoy while we walk this earth. Amen.

Lightening Our Load

'Come to me, all you that are weary and are carrying heavy burdens, and I will give you rest.
Take my yoke upon you, and learn from me;
for I am gentle and humble in heart,
and you will find rest for your souls.
For my yoke is easy, and my burden is light.'
~ ***Matthew 11:28-30***

Boy, was I tired! I didn't know if it was the weather switching back and forth so radically, or the early mornings with the late meetings, or just everyday stress. It may even have been a combination of all three. Whatever it was, I needed a nap!

Jesus told us that we don't have to face our wearying loads on our own. We can look to Him to help us carry the load by putting His "yoke upon" us. He helps to carry the day to day issues that can drag us down mentally and physically. When two share in carrying anything heavy, the burden is lightened and can be taken care of much easier than trying to deal with things on our own.

Take your everyday stress and issues to Jesus in prayer. He will "pick up" the other end of your load and help you through whatever you are dealing with. You never have to carry the load alone. Then you can finally find some much needed rest from all that has weighed you down when you were dealing with it alone.

Prayer

Dearest Lord Jesus, thank you for always being willing to "lighten our load" by "picking up the other end" and helping us carry on through whatever we are dealing with. Thank you for the rest we find in You once we allow You to join in on dealing with our everyday issues and stresses so that we never have to go it alone. Amen.

BLOWING IN THE WIND

The gifts he gave were that some would be apostles,
some prophets, some evangelists,
some pastors and teachers,
to equip the saints for the work of ministry,
for building up the body of Christ,
until all of us come to the unity of the faith
and of the knowledge of the Son of God, to maturity,
to the measure of the full stature of Christ.
We must no longer be children,
tossed to and fro and blown about by every wind of doctrine,
by people's trickery, by their craftiness in deceitful
scheming.
But speaking the truth in love,
we must grow up in every way into him who is the head,
into Christ, from whom the whole body,
joined and knitted together by every ligament
with which it is equipped, as each part is working properly,
promotes the body's growth in building itself up in love.
~ Ephesians 4:11-16

As I watched through the window, I saw the cold winds of January blowing the treetops to and fro, strongly enough that it looked as though the fragile, bare twigs should be snapped off in the swift gale. The snow swirled up off of the rooftops as well as the ground and wafted through the air like a white cloud of powder until coming in contact with an unmoving object, causing the flakes to fall at the base of the stationary mass, creating a drift that continued to grow in size. With a drift in the wake of a traveler, this could create havoc getting from one place to another.

Our lives can be much like the wind. The chaos of finding our spiritual gifts that leave our lives filling fulfilled are difficult to discern with the demands of today's society pulling us in all directions, trying to take up all of our time. Trying to just take a moment to quiet our inner thoughts to think about what really makes us feel like we are doing something worthwhile in the eyes of God is like an item on a "honey do" list...rarely getting to it when it needs to be done.

Tomorrow, our church family will have just such an opportunity to stand still and find just what their spiritual gifts may be. They will have a chance to learn more about the different avenues in which our church offers hands-on ministries that may help fulfill their desire to serve God by serving others. There are many avenues in which to do just that, and by matching the spiritual gifts of each person with opportunities to serve, they will no longer have to just "flop in the wind" as to where they should serve because they are unsure of what ministries need what spiritual gifts. Instead, they can join right in where they are most comfortable in serving. They will no longer feel like they are struggling through "snow drifts," but can move right along, accomplishing great things for God and the advancement of His kingdom!

Prayer

Father in Heaven, help us to make the time to really look within ourselves to discover just what spiritual gifts you have blessed us with and then help us to become involved in ministries that use these very gifts to further Your kingdom. Amen.

Winter No More

Ascribe to the LORD, O families of the peoples,
ascribe to the LORD glory and strength.
Ascribe to the LORD the glory due his name;
bring an offering, and come before him.
Worship the LORD in holy splendor;
tremble before him, all the earth.
The world is firmly established; it shall never be moved.
Let the heavens be glad, and let the earth rejoice,
and let them say among the nations, 'The LORD is king!'
Let the sea roar, and all that fills it;
let the field exult, and everything in it.
Then shall the trees of the forest sing for joy
before the LORD, for he comes to judge the earth.
O give thanks to the LORD, for he is good;
for his steadfast love endures forever.
~ 1 Chronicles 16:28-34

What a LONGGGGG winter we had had. I heard the cutest comments in an ad on the radio about what people may have done or said during the winter from being held captive by the cold and snow for so long. One man in the ad stated that he had knocked the head off of the neighbor's snowman, because he felt it was looking at him! Another was a woman saying she made not so nice comments to the weatherman while he gave the weather forecast on TV (and in person). This ad went on to say that, now that the weather was warming up, they could invite the neighbor and weatherman over for a barbecue.

I tuned out of the message at that point, with other things on my mind. I saw the grass turning greener and the leaf buds on the trees beginning to swell. The crocuses on the church grounds are blooming and my tulips and daffodils are poking through the ground. Spring is coming, although not as soon as I had wanted after this past winter. I am beginning to see the glory of God springing forth with new life once again. I rejoice that better weather is around the corner and I am finally seeing the first glimpses of it in these few signs of blooming and growth.

How often do we grumble and groan about where our life is at present or what we are having to go through that others do not? How do we rejoice during the good times? Do we tend to treat others with disdain when we are not happy and then turn around and celebrate happy times with them later? It is so very typical of human nature to do just that. God's people rejoiced in seeing Christ riding in on a donkey to Jerusalem, thinking that He was going to save them from the tyranny of Rome. They turned on Him in a matter of just a few days, when they realized that He was not going to save them as They thought He would. They jeered and mocked him - calling for His crucifixion just days after lauding Him as their King! After seeing His risen form, his disciples proclaimed to all who would hear that Christ is still alive and has made a way for us to God and eternal life if we repent and believe in Him. We again can celebrate this new life offered freely to us all.

Jesus has overcome the ultimate end called "death" and has broken a new path to eternal life. We are no longer judged by what we have repented of, for Christ paid for those sins long ago. We just need to remember to praise Him for all He has done for us and declare Him the King of our lives - serving Him wherever He leads us - and not continue in our old ways, which continue to bring Him heartache for those He loves so dearly. With Christ, our "winters" are over, for we will inherit the eternal life that will "spring" from our faith in Jesus.

Prayer

Dearest Lord Jesus, thank you for all you have given us - the beauty of the earth, the ever-renewing life around us, and most importantly, for saving us from death through Your overcoming death on a cross so that we can one day join You in heaven, praising our Heavenly Father for all eternity. Amen.

Finding the Path

I will lead the blind
by a road they do not know,
by paths they have not known
I will guide them.
I will turn the darkness before them into light,
the rough places into level ground.
These are the things I will do,
and I will not forsake them.
*~ **Isaiah 42:16***

Looking into the mounds of snow in the ravine, I see many types of tracks leading this way and that from different types of animals having traveled through the wooded area within the past day. With snow coming on the wind tomorrow, those tracks will soon be covered over. If a human were to have traveled those very paths and expected those tracks to remain there to lead them home at a later date, they would be in a sad situation had this been a wilderness area and the wind and snow came to cover their trail before they traveled home.

We, as Christians, don't need to worry about the "winds" of sin and deception coming to hide our pathway to God. He has provided a light and a map through His Word for us to follow to find our way back to Him, no matter where we may have wandered in our everyday lives. God will never allow us to remain lost if we truly seek Him. He may have us follow a path we never realized existed or that we have dreaded taking to finally get to Him, but He will never leave us stranded and alone. He is always ready to shine the light to lead us back to Him.

Prayer

Heavenly Father, when our lives seem lost and alone, help us to always look to You for guidance to get back on the pathway that leads home to You. Amen.

Wild Hairs

With my whole heart I seek you;
do not let me stray from your commandments.
~ Psalm 119:10

Some mornings, as I prepare to get ready, I find that I have a few areas of hair that refuse to be curled in the right direction. I keep rolling those areas under, only to find that they flip right back out! Sometimes it gets down right aggravating!

Areas of our Christian lives can be this way too. No matter how closely we try to walk with God, we find that "wild hairs" pop up and refuse to be put in their place. Perhaps these are old habits that are hard to break, just a whim of wanting to let go to child-like abandon, or things that we just really do not want to give up in our lives, but try to "sweep into our stocking cap" so nobody else sees them. The problem with this is, that no matter who we may hide our "wild hairs" from, God sees them all - even "in our stocking caps."

Just like a lot of hair spray and perseverance may eventually tame the wild hairs seen in the morning mirror, a lot of heart-felt prayer and soul searching can produce the outcome we know God would like to see in our spiritual lives to get rid of our wild hairs we know we should definitely tame into submission.
What "wild hairs" do you have in your life that need taming? Search your soul and pray to God in sincere earnest to help you bring these things under control. You will feel at peace once you do!

Prayer

Lord, we know that, to grow closer to You, we need to "tame" our "wild hairs" in a way that allows us to live our lives reflecting Your love to all those around us. Help us to no longer desire the things that pull us away from You. We know we can overcome all things with You beside us. Amen.

UNCONDITIONAL LOVE

'You have heard that it was said,
"You shall love your neighbor and hate your enemy."
But I say to you, Love your enemies
and pray for those who persecute you,
so that you may be children of your Father in heaven;
for he makes his sun rise on the evil and on the good,
and sends rain on the righteous and on the unrighteous.
For if you love those who love you,
what reward do you have?
Do not even the tax-collectors do the same?
And if you greet only your brothers and sisters,
what more are you doing than others?
Do not even the Gentiles do the same? Be perfect,
therefore, as your heavenly Father is perfect.
*~ **Matthew 5:43-48***

There are five types of "love" that are written about in the Bible. Mania, which hinges on obsession toward someone. Eros, which is an emotional attachment to someone. Philos, which is brotherly love or friendship. Storgy, which is like parental love toward a dependent. Last, but not least, the one most talked about in the Bible - Agape, which is concentrates on being given freely to all, like charity - even to our enemies.

God loves each and every one of us so completely, that He gave His one and only Son to die for all that we do wrong so that we have access to Him directly and have a relationship with Him as a father to his child. He did this before He even created us, knowing that in order for us to be able to come before Him, pure and blameless, we would need to have had our sins paid for through the blood of the ultimate sacrifice. Since He has loved us so completely before we were even brought into being, should we not also love as God loves? This is how He wishes for us to love - to love even those that seem not worth loving - our very enemies.

Who do you tend to ignore and despise? Rethink how God views these same people and show the love of God to all - through prayer and actions - so that your works may be an offering to God for the unconditional love He has bestowed on us all. Through your unconditional love to even your worst enemy, you will become a blessing from God to all who encounter you.

Prayer

Lord, fill me and use me as an instrument of your peace. Where there is hate, help me sow love - no matter how difficult the situation may be - so that all who see me may see Your light shining through me. Amen.

Soak It In and Grow

Ground that drinks up the rain falling on it repeatedly,
and that produces a crop useful
to those for whom it is cultivated,
receives a blessing from God.
~ Hebrews 6:7

After what seemed to have been an extra-long winter of too much snow, we were seeing the first signs of spring trying to burst forth with warmer weather and rain to melt the residual snows that still remained all around us. The winds were blowing strongly on this sunny February day, much like we are used to seeing in March. The ditches and ravines were running with cool streams of melted snows once again, lined by white blankets of snow that refuse to join in the travel of the streams they line. The ground was saturated with water, but this very ground would soon produce the beautiful, lush carpets of green grass that we were so looking forward to after having seen so much white for so long.

God's Word is like the spring rains and melting snows of winter. It falls upon our ears in worship service or is absorbed into our minds as we read it. What we learn from His Word helps to produce good works on His behalf to others all around us. The good works that we do in His name become blessings in return for us, as we feel the satisfaction of doing good for others. If fills us with a sense of purpose and accomplishment that show us that we have an important part to play in the world today, as well as into the future.

Our church will be examining areas of spiritual gifts and ministries within our church that our church family can become involved in. These ministries help to bring fulfillment to lives that are looking for ways to serve God, as well as to those needing these very ministries to fill their spirits with God's love. Ministries can be as simple as volunteering in a church office, helping with mailings, or delivering items to food pantries. They can be as involved as joining in a mission trip to serve elsewhere or serve at a food kitchen. Whatever and wherever one of the family of God finds meaning and purpose to fulfill God's mission in their lives, it can be found by exploring the different opportunities within the church. From there, they can branch out to even more areas outside of the church to serve a greater need for those not here yet - those still seeking after God and not yet having found Him.

What are your spiritual gifts? How can you live a more fulfilled life in service to God? Come explore ways to serve that you may not have even thought of and grow in your faith as you do the work of our Lord.

Prayer

Lord, may Your Word guide me and show me how to better serve You, so that my faith in You will grow and blossom into all that You have put me here to be. Amen.

OUTSIDERS VS. INSIDERS

*On the Sabbath he began to teach in the synagogue,
and many who heard him were astounded.
They said, 'Where did this man get all this?
What is this wisdom that has been given to him?
What deeds of power are being done by his hands!
Is not this the carpenter, the son of Mary
and brother of James and Joses and Judas and Simon,
and are not his sisters here with us?' And they took offense
at him. Then Jesus said to them, 'Prophets are not without
honor, except in their home town, and among their own kin,
and in their own house.'
And he could do no deed of power there, except that he
laid his hands on a few sick people and cured them.
And he was amazed at their unbelief.*
~ Mark 6:2-5

A famous person is not always viewed by their family the same way outsiders view them. Having watched the person adored by outsiders grow up, family members have seen another side of this person that outsiders have never seen. Outsiders only view what the media allows them to see or hear about and make their decisions based on what is happening in the life of this person now, not necessarily what has happened to them in their past. Insiders remember the person growing up and cannot always separate their close relationship and past from what the person has become.

Jesus had much the same trouble with his own family and small hometown. They knew this young man as he had grown up in the community. It was difficult for them to separate the fact that Jesus was both human and divine. They had never experienced such a thing before, so how could they believe that Jesus was more than just a man? Had he not been born of a woman as they had been? Had he not grown up much like they had, in this small community of people that knew everyone and everything everyone ever did in this little town?

Being and outsider can sometimes be a good thing, for they are able to see things that those in an inner circle may not. Outsiders are not taking things for granted, for they are seeing these things for the very first time. They are making decisions based on what is happening at the moment, not allowing previous knowledge cloud their ability to see what is right in front of their eyes.

By being outsiders, we have the ability to see what God has intended for everyone to see - that Jesus was God in the flesh, walking this very same earth we live in and showing us how we should live our lives to please Him. As outsiders, we are not looking at Jesus as if he were our sibling that could do no wrong in our mother's eyes. We can see Him as a Healer and eventually a Savior, who became the very sacrificial lamb saving us from all we have done wrong in our lives by believing in Him.

What do you see when you look to Jesus? Do you see just a man having walked this earth as we do now? Or do you see Jesus as the Son of God who not only died for us, but still walks among us every day?

Prayer

Dearest Lord Jesus, let us not take You for granted. Thank You for having walked this earth as an example of how to live our lives in the way that honors God. Thank You for still walking with us today, every step of the way, so that we are never alone in this world. Amen.

PRAY WITHOUT CEASING

Rejoice always, pray without ceasing, give thanks
in all circumstances;
for this is the will of God in Christ Jesus for you.
~ 1 Thessalonians 5:16-18

Watching out my kitchen window, like most mornings in the winter, I watched the three squirrels that frequent the ground just under the bird feeder. They sat on their little haunches, bending over and sitting back up quickly to devour whatever little morsel they had found discarded by the birds above, then quickly repeated the action for as long as they were undisturbed by humans or until they had had their fill. When they ate, they always looked like they were saying a short prayer for each bite they took.

This made me think about how often I lift a prayer of thanksgiving up to God throughout the day for what I have been given or am experiencing. I saw that, through the actions of a squirrel looking like it was praying over each morsel, a tiny animal may appear more grateful to God than I sometimes seem to Him. I often take things for granted - my home, what I have to eat, my job, my family and friends. I saw that I say very few actual prayers throughout the day. Usually I do at mealtime and maybe just before I fall asleep, but throughout the entire day? No.

Perhaps, though, prayer isn't always given in words to God. Perhaps, it is partly how we live our lives in response to our gifts that are also considered "praying without ceasing." If we live our life in a manner that reflects our gratitude through sharing what we have with others, showing our faith in God through all circumstances - good and bad, and giving God the credit for all we have and are able to do, maybe - just maybe - that is part of what "praying without ceasing" is all about.

Are you grateful for all you have been given from God? Even when times are not how you would like them to be? Continue to "pray without ceasing" by living a life of thanksgiving and praise to Him at all times, as well as actual verbal prayers. In this way, God will see that you are also as grateful, if not more so, than the squirrels that gather under the bird feeder.

Prayer

Lord, I know that I often appear "ungrateful" or take for granted what You have blessed me with. I also know that You are always with me - in good times and bad. Please, help me to always show the love and appreciation for all of Your gifts You have given me through the way I live my life. May how I live my life appear to others as an "unceasing prayer to You" and through this, draw them to You as well. Amen.

SURPRISE BLESSINGS

I pray that the God of our Lord Jesus Christ,
the Father of glory,
may give you a spirit of wisdom and revelation
as you come to know him,
so that, with the eyes of your heart enlightened,
you may know what is the hope to which he has called you,
what are the riches of his glorious inheritance
among the saints, and what is the immeasurable greatness
of his power for us who believe,
according to the working of his great power.
*~ **Ephesians 1:17-19***

A man who likes to make videos that go "viral" on U-Tube recently learned that a surprise blessing given may turn around and bless you back in return. He arranged with a local merchant to have a "winning lottery ticket" payoff of $1,000 be made for a phony lottery ticket that he would give to a homeless man, so that he could give this homeless man that amount of money anonymously. He would then direct to this homeless man to this merchant's store to see if it was a winner. The man planning this whole thing would have a camera set up to catch the reaction of the homeless man collecting the "winnings" of this gifted ticket.

When the homeless man "cashed in" his "winning ticket" and he learned of how much he had won, his first response was to turn to the man that had given him the ticket and offered to share the winnings with him. The gifter of the ticket was so taken aback by this reaction that he was moved to tears and hugged the homeless man for his unselfish response to his "windfall." A man that had nothing was ready to share with someone that had so much more.

How often do we think about what we have in comparison to others? How much are we willing to give up to make someone else happier around us? How much do we take for granted what God has blessed us with? It is never too late to have a revelation of what our blessings are and how we can share those blessings with others around us, so that our gifts may glorify God and bring others to the knowledge of His greatness.

Prayer

Dear Father in Heaven, thank you for all you have blessed me with. May I always be ready to share these many blessings with others so that, through my generosity of sharing Your many blessings, they may also be drawn to You. Amen

IN DUE SEASON

Can you lead forth the Mazzaroth in their season,
or can you guide the Bear with its children?
*~ **Job 38:32***

It was the first day of spring, although it was hard to believe that the season had really arrived, with the few scattered snow flakes that greeted me as I walked out the door to go to work that morning. The sky was still gray and depressing, and the grass still brown, although still covered here and there with remnants of snow drifts from the winter that did not want to leave just yet.

The sun did eventually fight its way through the clouds by late morning to show that there is a hint of spring in the light of the sun with grass trying to change to its prettier green color. Just as we cannot control the constellations in the sky, neither can we control the seasons just because what we label "the first day of spring" has arrived.

We, as Christians, go through seasons as well. There are times we are on fire with the Holy Spirit, accomplishing all sorts of good things in the name of our Lord. There are other days where we seem dormant in our faith, like it is hibernating or stagnant. God has us all here for a purpose and our purpose may not always be to be on fire. We may have times that we are just here to help others along behind the scenes when times get tough. Whatever God's purpose is for us, He determines when and how to use us.

Are you ready to feel God's gentle tug on your sleeve to do His work at His timing? Are you expecting to be on fire all of the time? Remember, whatever His purpose for you is, He will use you when and where He needs you.

Prayer

Father in Heaven, we do not always know exactly what it is You wish for us to do in Your name, or when to do it. Help us to always be aware of and ready to follow Your urging to do Your bidding at the times You need us to do them. Amen.

GOD'S POWER IN OUR LIVES

So it depends not on human will or exertion,
but on God who shows mercy.
For the scripture says to Pharaoh, '
I have raised you up for the very purpose
of showing my power in you,
so that my name may be proclaimed in all the earth.'
*~ **Romans 9:16-17***

Sometimes we see situations that we try to handle on our own. Maybe we feel that we can handle it ourselves instead of bothering God with the problem, because we feel He has bigger, more important things to attend to. After a time of trying to fix the problem on our own, we realize that, "no, God will have to handle this after all."

God doesn't expect us to handle things on our own. He is always with us, ready to take our hand and guide us through whatever we are dealing with. He doesn't want us to face things on our own. He is our Father and wants the very best for us, but like allowing a toddler to just experience some newfound freedom to explore on our own, he allows us to come to the realization that we need God's help without Him demanding to step in and help us. It is a learning experience for us throughout our lives. We see God's power in our lives when we let go and allow Him to lead and work His power to solve our difficulties for us.

What isn't going quite right in your life right now? Can you hand it over to God and watch Him work a miracle before your eyes? He's waiting for you to ask.

Prayer

Father in Heaven, thank you for allowing us the freedom to explore what we can and cannot do on our own. Help us to always remember not to allow ourselves to get frustrated in not being able to solve all of our own problems on our own, but rather to lean on You for our ultimate help in time of need. Amen.

MIRACLES THROUGH CHILDREN

Now the Passover, the festival of the Jews, was near.
When he looked up and saw a large crowd
coming towards him, Jesus said to Philip,
'Where are we to buy bread for these people to eat?'
He said this to test him, for he himself knew what he was
going to do. Philip answered him,
'Six months' wages would not buy enough bread
for each of them to get a little.'
One of his disciples, Andrew,
Simon Peter's brother, said to him,
'There is a boy here who has five barley loaves and two fish.
But what are they among so many people?'
Jesus said, 'Make the people sit down.'
Now there was a great deal of grass in the place;
so they sat down, about five thousand in all.
Then Jesus took the loaves, and when he had given thanks,
he distributed them to those who were seated; so also the
fish, as much as they wanted. When they were satisfied,
he told his disciples, 'Gather up the fragments left over,
so that nothing may be lost.' So they gathered them up,
and from the fragments of the five barley loaves, left by those
who had eaten, they filled twelve baskets.
When the people saw the sign that he had done,
they began to say,
'This is indeed the prophet who is to come into the world.'
~ *John 6:4-14*

One year, our Vacation Bible School project offerings were designated to the "No More Malaria" project. Malaria is a disease transmitted by mosquitoes that was wiped out in the United States in the 1950's, yet one child or mother in

Africa still dies every minute in Africa today. Our church had pledged to raise funds over the next three years to go to the "No More Malaria" campaign to help wipe out malaria in Africa.

Over the course of the year, several fund-raising projects had been planned to work toward our church's pledge goal. One of these was a goal of $300 from VBS offerings. We were amazed at just how powerfully the story of the dangers of mosquitoes affected the hearts of the children attending Vacation Bible School. Some went right out and started to raise money in various ways to bring in for the offering the next day. One had a lemonade stand, a couple of others sold glow stick necklaces at the theater, etc. These children really wanted to make a difference for children and mothers in Africa. Each day, the total offering for the day increased significantly. By the third day, they had more than reached their goal, but they still weren't done! They went out and almost doubled their total for three days on day four! They had raised $750 on their own by the close of VBS on Thursday. One generous donor, seeing what the children had raised on their own, made up the difference and donated enough to put the children over the $1,000 mark! Still, parents and children were still giving at the end of the day, so the total has grown even more, with a final program tonight most assuredly topping off the figure even higher.

Just like the little boy with the bread and fish given to Jesus to feed the multitude, God has used the hearts of these children that have come through our doors to make a difference in the lives of others half way around the world. The multiplying of their generosity has more than tripled the original goal for this mission project for the four-day Vacation Bible School program. They are still spreading the word for others to get involved as well, so that malaria can be wiped out for everyone.

How can you help? You can go to our website and donate to UMCOR through our church. So many senseless deaths occur every day from a disease that is 100% curable if only people could have access to the medication needed to heal them from this mosquito-born illness. The time to help is now. Will you help save a life by giving as these young children have this week?

Prayer

Dear Lord, thank you for the many blessings that children remind us of everyday. Their open hearts and love for others less fortunate are examples that we, as adults, need to remember and follow every day to help bring the necessary changes for a better tomorrow all around the world. Amen.

WONDROUS LOVE

Then Pilate took Jesus and had him flogged.
And the soldiers wove a crown of thorns
and put it on his head,
and they dressed him in a purple robe.
They kept coming up to him, saying, '
Hail, King of the Jews!'
and striking him on the face.
Pilate went out again and said to them,
'Look, I am bringing him out to you to let you know
that I find no case against him.'
So Jesus came out, wearing the crown of thorns
and the purple robe. Pilate said to them, 'Here is the man!'
When the chief priests and the police saw him, they shouted,
'Crucify him! Crucify him!' Pilate said to them, 'Take him
yourselves and crucify him; I find no case against him.'
*~ **John 19:1-6***

Good Friday always makes me reflect on that Holy Day, so very long ago, where the only perfect man to have lived upon this earth chose to go through unthinkable torture and death to save someone like me.   To hear of the actual pain that Christ had to endure for me brings me to tears. Watching the movie, ***"The Passion of Christ,"*** really brought it all home a few years ago in a very visual representation of what I, and everyone else, should have had to endure at life's end for all of our sinful ways. Every blow of the whip made me cringe. The taunting, beating and spitting upon Christ was so unfair. Yet, Jesus took all this upon Himself so that none of us will ever have to endure such pain to pay the price of our own sin if we believe in Him.

The whipping, beating, taunting and spitting upon Jesus wasn't even the worst of the punishment. Sweating blood from His terrible beating earlier in the day, He still had to carry His cross up a winding hill to the place of His ultimate death. The soldiers nailed Him to the cross through His feet and hands, (although it is now said that it was probably through His wrist at the base of His hand). Then to have to hang for three hours, with His already bloody, beaten back rubbing agonizingly against the rough post as He put pressure on His feet to raise Himself up enough to draw a breath of air, then slide back down the post again to have the pressure of His weight pulling at the nails at His hands prolonged the feeling of the previous beating. All the while, His lungs are filling with fluid, making it harder and harder to breath as He slowly suffocated in His own body fluid.

Through all of this pain and torture, Jesus still made the time to see that His mother would be cared for, forgave those who persecuted Him, "for they know not what they are doing," and tells a thief that is dying beside Him that he "will be with me in paradise," for this one thief already could see that Jesus did not deserve to die, for He had done nothing wrong. This thief, instead, rebukes the other thief who is taunting Jesus from his own cross of death, and asks Jesus to remember him when He comes into His kingdom. This is proof that, even if we are so stubborn as to not see Christ for who He really is until almost our final moment here on earth, it is never too late to ask for forgiveness and believe in Him. Christ will still forgive us and take us to be with Him for all eternity.

Really think about the pain that Christ suffered to save you with His unfathomable love for each and everyone of us. How many people that love you now would be willing to undergo so much pain and agony to save you? Would you be willing to undergo that kind of torture for others you love? Even for those that have wronged you in so many ways? May a deeper realization of just how much Jesus loves you be gained as you meditate on Christ and His ultimate sacrifice to save you from eternal death.

Prayer

Dearest Lord Jesus, as I ponder the cross and all that it represents for me and everyone else, I am drawn to tears by how deep Your love is for each and every one of us to have endured so much pain, torture and ridicule just to save me. I know I have done nothing to deserve Your love or greatest sacrifice on my behalf, but I thank You and praise You for loving me so much that You did undergo the cross and death to save a sinful creature like me. Amen.

Easter Isn't Over

But in fact Christ has been raised from the dead,
the first fruits of those who have died.
For since death came through a human being,
the resurrection of the dead
has also come through a human being;
for as all die in Adam, so all will be made alive in Christ.
But each in his own order: Christ the first fruits,
then at his coming those who belong to Christ.
~ 1 Corinthians 15:20-23

Easter has come once again! A reminder that all things are made new through Christ our Lord and Savior! Life everlasting is available for all who believe in Him. What a joyous message! This message, however, is not a "one time only" sort of message throughout the year, but one that is for all time!

Adam and Eve had condemned us all to death due to that first sin in the beginning of time. Sin came through one woman and one man into this world. People atoned for their sins for hundreds of years after, through blood sacrifice of animals and offering the first fruits of their harvests. Only the sacrifice of one perfect man would really set us free once and for all!

Jesus took it upon Himself to leave His throne in heaven to dwell among us. He suffered right along with us as He experienced pain and loss as we do. He also celebrated great joys throughout His time among us. He loved us so much, that He willingly went through the harshest punishment known to man in His time that ended in His earthly death - a death from which no one had ever returned before. Jesus, however, was the Almighty God incarnate and had the power to overcome death so that we too may live again in glory with Him one day! Easter is not over! Easter has only just begun!

Prayer

Dearest Lord Jesus, thank you for loving us so much that You paid the ultimate price so that we might live eternally with You. May our praises never cease as we give You our unending gratitude and love. Amen.

POWER OF PRAYER

The prayer of faith will save the sick,
and the Lord will raise them up;
and anyone who has committed sins will be forgiven.
Therefore confess your sins to one another,
and pray for one another, so that you may be healed.
The prayer of the righteous is powerful and effective.
*~ **James 5:15-16***

I know I have written about the power of prayer before, but once again, I have heard of the miracle of prayer within just the last few weeks. An older cousin of mine, who lives out of state, posted a request for prayers on Facebook for his daughter, who had been hit by a semi while riding her scooter. His first pleas for prayer gave us reason to worry that perhaps this young woman might not make it.

Further on in the request, however, he was already praising God's miraculous intervention in that her scooter had been flattened and she had not been hit by the vehicle itself, but sustained broken ribs, lots of road rash and a head injury. Even before a prayer was lifted for God's healing grace, God had already saved her from what could have been certain death. This answer to unsaid specific prayer may have been from earlier prayers of protection for her that were said and forgotten about by the one praying for her safety, but was not forgotten by God.

More miracles continued in the coming two weeks of Melissa's healing process. Her open wounds to her head and road rash areas healed over quickly, despite the first prognosis that skin grafts would probably be needed. Her mother took a leave of absence from work, expecting to continue caring for Melissa at home over a period of 8-10 weeks. Within two weeks, Melissa has healed leaps and bounds - much more quickly than ever thought possible by the doctors. She was walking around under her own power, had just gotten the 15 staples removed from her scalp and, although still very tender in the ribs, has recovered quite well in these past two weeks!

There are many people that wonder if miracles still happen, or if God really answers prayers. I have seen too many instances in just the past few years to know that God is very much alive and still working miracles every day. We just have to look around and pay attention to what it going on around us. Continue to pray for those close to you as well as the stranger on the street. God is hearing each and every prayer and answering them just as He always has. We just are not always aware of just how powerful and effective our prayer life is and what a difference it is making in someone else's life.

Prayer

Dear Heavenly Father, we do not always think that our prayers matter, when each and every one said to You means far more to You than we think it might. Thank You for the many answers to prayers and miracles that You continue to perform right before our very eyes. Amen.

God's Glory Shining Through Our Weakness

Therefore, to keep me from being too elated,
a thorn was given to me in the flesh,
a messenger of Satan to torment me,
to keep me from being too elated.
Three times I appealed to the Lord about this,
that it would leave me, but he said to me, '
My grace is sufficient for you,
for power is made perfect in weakness.'
So, I will boast all the more gladly of my weaknesses,
so that the power of Christ may dwell in me.
Therefore I am content with weaknesses,
insults, hardships, persecutions,
and calamities for the sake of Christ;
for whenever I am weak, then I am strong.
*~ **2 Corinthians 12:7b-10***

Oh, this weather is difficult on the body as we get older. As the damp, dreary days continue, so do the traveling aches and pains from joint to joint. It is literally a "pain" getting older!

Paul, during his ministry, endured many beatings - almost to the point of death at times. With each beating, his physical body became weaker, yet his faith in God through Christ Jesus continued to grow stronger. God's glory could be seen through Paul's many trials and hardships, for not only did his faith grow, but so did the Christian church throughout the lands. He was willing to suffer, if that was what he must do, to help spread the gospel of Christ throughout the known world. He chose to continue his ministry, despite the fact that God did not remove the afflictions from him as he requested through repeated prayers.

We, today, still have many afflictions and events that may try to pull our faith away from God due to prayers not being answered as we would like them to be. We may continue to have aches, pains, illnesses, financial difficulties, etc., but we can still use these difficulties in our lives to let our faith and love of God through Jesus Christ continue to shine forth from us for others to see. Our continued faith, even during times of adversity, may be just what someone else needs to see. Perhaps this is just what will lead them to a relationship with Christ - the continued joy and devotion of those going through difficult times to the One who controls all things to be used for His glory.

Prayer

Lord, we all dislike going through difficult times. Some of us seem to go through more than others. Help us to continue to let our love-light for You shine forth, even in our darkest situations, so that others that do not know You may come to see that a relationship with You is worth more than anything this world can possibly throw our way. Amen.

WOMEN SERVING GOD ARE A BLESSING

Charm is deceitful, and beauty is vain,
but a woman who fears the Lord is to be praised.
*~ **Proverbs 31:30***

When I was growing up, I always wanted to be just like my mom. I thought she was not only beautiful of face, but in spirit as well. She was always up before anyone else, making breakfast to get us all out the door for work or school on time, kept the house clean and had regular meals on the table every evening. She always showed her love for us in all she did. On Sundays, she not only taught Sunday school at our small rural church, but picked up the neighborhood kids to take with us, because their parents were not church goers.

To me, my mother was a "saint" that I wanted to emulate later in life. My fiery temper and quick tongue, however, were not like my mother. I struggled with that part of my personality that was so in conflict with who I wanted to be as I got older. To this day, I still struggle with it, though most people who see me outside the home cannot usually picture me with such a problem. Working in a church office has helped calm that part of me down a bit, but even then, I have my moments, as all humans do.

God knows that we are not perfect, but when we strive to do work to further His kingdom, all those around us see the "beauty" of His grace and love shining into the lives of those we serve. Like my mother, women that work to help others grow in their faith or serve others on a daily basis out of love through Christ are to be praised for their faithfulness and unselfishness. They show the love and support for others in all that they do - like a mother cares for her own children. Mothers Day is a wonderful day set aside to do just that. Even if a woman is not a mother physically, those she serves and cares for like a mother make her one to be honored among women. Remember to thank these women in your life as well as your own mother this Sunday. God has put them in your life to show His love to you through them.

Prayer

Heavenly Father, thank you for all of the women You have placed in our lives to show us Your love and care. Be they our physical mother or someone else that shows us the way that leads to You, please bless them for their faithfulness in serving you. Amen.

Peace for Our Souls

For the mountains may depart
and the hills be removed,
but my steadfast love shall not depart from you,
and my covenant of peace shall not be removed,
says the Lord, who has compassion on you.
*~ **Isaiah 54:10***

One morning, I heard a storm moving in - the rain beating down on the roof as I waited to leave for work. I had hoped that it would lighten up by the time I needed to leave, but instead, it continued to beat heavily. As I finally looked out the window, the rain was coming down in heavy sheets, with the wind blowing it sideways. I decided I could wait no longer, as I would already be a few minutes late. There did not appear to be a break in sight.

Dashing the 5 yards or so to my vehicle, I was immediately drenched! As much as I hate to run the wipers, I had no choice this morning, for I could not see out of my windshield with the amount of water running across it. The ditches could not handle the rain as quickly as it was coming down, so the water on the road also became a hazard to contend with. A few miles down the road, the rain started to let up to a more manageable pattering and by the time I arrived at the church, I didn't have to worry so much about another drenching as I walked from my vehicle to open up the doors, still very damp from my initial soaking.

Once inside, a sense of peace settled upon me, knowing that I was safely at work once again in the house of the Lord. Grabbing a cup of coffee, I settled in to my usual routine for a Friday morning of sending out the UPDATE e-mail to parishioners for the week's coming events. Looking out the window, I saw the stream racing by in the wooded area just to the east of the church.

Life is much like that racing stream and stormy downpour, I thought. We dread going out into the tumult of life that seems to speed by us at lightning speed. We are afraid of being "drenched" in the difficulties that lie ahead of us. Before we know it, weeks and years have passed by us. Just what have we accomplished in the chaos that we call life? Where is that sense of peace that we want to find shelter in from the storm?

Until we find our shelter in the Lord, we will not find that sense of peace that we long for in life. Knowing that "all is well" is so comforting. God will always welcome us in from the storms that surround us to bring us that peace we seek. Then we can join in the all-familiar tune, "*It is Well with My Soul*."

Prayer

Father in Heaven, thank You for being our shelter in the storms of life. Thank You for the peace You bring us when we seek and finally find You. You are our safe haven - making all well within our souls. Amen.

Revealing God's Wondrous Works

My soul clings to the dust;
revive me according to your word.
When I told of my ways, you answered me;
teach me your statutes.
Make me understand the way of your precepts,
and I will meditate on your wondrous works.
*~ **Psalm 119:25-27***

After the rains of the past weekend, the greenery in the stream bed alongside of the church hads become a jungle of tall plants and trees popping into fullness with their new leaves. I stared *in* awe at how quickly God's plants changed from slight signs of spring to full blossom in a matter of just a few days time. The waters quietly meandered through the stream bed and on down the hill, while small wildlife showed their heads now and again while running through the new plant life or flitted from branch to branch among the trees.

Meditating on God's Word, just as we meditate on His creation, we can also become awestruck by the history of His creation from the very beginning of time. God has had a purpose throughout all eternity for everything He has created - including us. He reveals His love throughout His written Word for us to find and share with others.
We have only to take the time to commune with God for Him to teach us of all of His wondrous works that He has done to show His unending love and yearning for us to have a close relationship with Him. From the time of Adam and Eve, God shows us how much He loves us all by eventually having His only begotten Son become the ultimate sacrifice to reconcile us to Him. This amazing sacrifice allows our relationship with

Him to blossom into an eternal life with Him one day. God's word shows the wondrous works of His hands - all done in love for us.

Prayer

Lord, looking around us, we see the handiwork of all Your creation and the beauty that it gives this earth. Help us to also find the handiwork and beauty within Your Holy Word as we read and meditate on it. Reveal to us just exactly what You want us to learn and apply to our lives so that we shine Your light for everyone to see. Amen.

Eternal and Living Guidance

Indeed, the word of God is living and active,
sharper than any two-edged sword,
piercing until it divides soul from spirit, joints from marrow;
it is able to judge the thoughts and intentions of the heart.
And before him no creature is hidden,
but all are naked and laid bare
to the eyes of the one to whom we must render an account.
~ Hebrews 4:12-13

Today's society is so very different than society back in biblical times. We often feel that, since many things we have available to us today didn't exist back then, that the Bible can't possibly address how we are to view things now. However, the Bible is God's Word. He is unchanging, as is all that He has said from the beginning of time.

Reading through the Word of God, we often seek to justify things that we feel should change, as times have obviously changed. God's Word will always cut through our desire to justify our behaviors today - showing us that our desires are not always in line with God's will. We are responsible for what we do today, just as our ancestors were hundreds of years before us. The game may have changed up a bit, but God's rules remain the same.

When in doubt as to how to live our lives according to the will of God, always seek His guidance through His Word and through prayer. He will reveal the direction we must go so that we will stay on His path instead of running off in our own direction that may lead away from Him. After all, we will be held accountable for the decisions we make while here on earth, so let us seek guidance from the One we are to please while we are here, and it is by His measure we will be judged in the end.

Prayer

God of the eternal ages, curb our selfish desires to do things our own way, which may detour us in the wrong direction for our lives. Let us always look to You for guidance through these constantly changing times so that we can clearly discern Your direction in our lives and stay on the path that leads to You and eternal life in Your kingdom. Amen.

CHILDREN OF FAITH

Everyone who believes that Jesus is the Christ
has been born of God,
and everyone who loves the parent loves the child.
By this we know that we love the children of God,
when we love God and obey his commandments.
For the love of God is this, that we obey his commandments.
And his commandments are not burdensome,
for whatever is born of God conquers the world.
And this is the victory that conquers the world, our faith.
~ 1 John 5:1-4

Most children love their parents unconditionally. Since we are human, there are always exceptions to this, but as a rule of thumb, you will find that most children will cling to their parents before clinging to someone else. Children put their trust in their parents, because they know that they will be taken care of - fed, clothed, housed, loved, protected from harm, etc.

When we believe in Christ as our Savior, we are become born of God. We love Him as we love a father who cares for his child. We want to please God by doing what He asks us to do, which is to obey His commandments, laid out for us when Moses met with God on mountain. These are not difficult commandments, although we always seem to break one here and there in our lives. This is why Jesus died for us - to pay for the times we fail to obey, even though we try our very hardest to follow the path to God.

Since Jesus paid the costly price for the many times that we do fail to show our love to God by falling away from His commandments and going on our own path, we have only repent and return to the path God has laid out so specifically for us. We are to show love to Him by loving others as we would want to be loved. In the end, we will conquer this temporary world through our faith by gaining the eternal life that awaits at the end of our earthly existence.

Prayer

Heavenly Father, when we see how easy it is to love and follow You, it seems difficult to believe that we often fall away to our own desires. Thank you for giving us the way to forgiveness and ability to return to You through Your Son, Jesus Christ, so that we can still be given our eternal relationship with You some day. Amen.

Taking Care of "Busy-ness"

What gain have the workers from their toil?
I have seen the business that God has given
to everyone to be busy with.
He has made everything suitable for its time; moreover,
he has put a sense of past and future into their minds,
yet they cannot find out what God has done
from the beginning to the end.
I know that there is nothing better for them than to be happy
and enjoy themselves as long as they live; moreover,
it is God's gift that all should eat and drink
and take pleasure in all their toil.
I know that whatever God does endures for ever;
nothing can be added to it, nor anything taken from it;
God has done this,
so that all should stand in awe before him.
~ Ecclesiastes 3:9-14

Lately, there just doesn't seem to be enough time in the day to get done all of the tasks that are at hand. There are deadlines to meet and that overlap with each other, vacation schedules to work around, "little surprises" that pop up to eat away at more of the time that should be devoted to other things. Life is just plain BUSY!

God has a time for everything. He wants us to enjoy our time here, even while we are busy "taking care of business." We cannot adjust anything God has already designed to have done, yet we go about our daily chores as if the world might just stop if we don't complete what we have set out to do. We often put undue stress on ourselves, because of these "deadlines" and the "busy-ness" we surround ourselves with.

When we are feeling just a bit overwhelmed with all that is filling our day, we need to just step back, inhale slowly, and look around at all that God has already done for us. By allowing ourselves to stop and just take in all that God has already accomplished and given us, we can breathe easy as we look in awe of His creation and all He provides, say a "thank you, Lord," and let the peace of His presence enter our souls to refresh and restore our minds and spirits. We may then go back to our work with renewed strength, knowing that all we do, we do out of love for our Heavenly Father, who provides us with all we need.

Prayer

Father in Heaven, thank you for times of rest and times of "busy-ness." Thank You for always providing for us even before we know what our needs are. Help us to enjoy the work You have set before us. May we glorify You in all that we do. Amen.

LET THE CHILDREN COME...

We will not hide them from their children;
we will tell to the coming generation
the glorious deeds of the LORD, and his might,
and the wonders that he has done.
*~ **Psalm 78:4***

Summer had come, and with it, another round of Vacation Bible School had just begun. I loved watching the eager faces of the children as they went from station to station experiencing the daily activities of the program. Our adult and youth volunteers put a lot of time, energy and creativity into each year's program to make the children have a memorable time as they learned about God and His love for them. So often, we hear from the parents as they are signing up their children for the coming event that their child had such a great time the previous year and that they were really looking forward to coming again this year, or that they planned their vacation time around the event so their child could attend.

God stated over and over again in His Word to train up the children to know of all His great works and love for them. He wants so much for all to know and have a personal relationship with Him. When a child is trained up in knowing about God and how He wants them to live, even if they deviate in their early adult years from His path, they are able to find their way back to Him much easier than coming to know Him for the first time as an adult. This is not to say that an adult cannot come to know the Lord, for this happens all of the time, but a child that has been raised in knowing about God will find that He is the answer they have been searching for when they come to the knowledge that something is missing from their life later on, due to the basic knowledge they learned about Him at an earlier age. Someone that has gone their entire childhood without knowing about God will still find Him, but He will not be one of the first paths they will search down to find the fulfillment that they need in their life.

We are so thankful to have so many wonderful volunteers willing to teach and lead the many children that have come through our church doors. They are truly blessings from the Lord. Their willingness to instill in these little ones the love and knowledge of God at a level the children can understand will be a starting point for many of them as they grow into adulthood and a closer relationship with Him.

Prayer

Dear Lord, thank you for the many people willing to instill in the young children of today the love and wondrous works You have done for them. May the children learning about You come to know You as the One Solid Foundation in which to place their trust and love. Amen.

CHRIST-LIKE ENCOURAGEMENT

If then there is any encouragement in Christ,
any consolation from love, any sharing in the Spirit,
any compassion and sympathy, make my joy complete:
be of the same mind, having the same love,
being in full accord and of one mind.
Do nothing from selfish ambition or conceit,
but in humility regard others as better than yourselves.
Let each of you look not to your own interests,
but to the interests of others.
Let the same mind be in you that was in Christ Jesus,
*~ **Philippians 2:1-5***

These days, it seems so few people are willing to step up and do things unless there is something in it for them. Everyone expects to get something in return for what they do in life. Each generation seems to get more and more into the "me" mentality.

I remember when I was growing up, people often volunteered to do things out of a desire to help others. Neighbors would step in and help each other when one of them was going through a difficult time, such as a severe illness or death of a loved one. Now, most people are so wrapped up in their own lives, they fail to notice others around them in need of a kind word, a little help to get through a difficult time, or even just a short prayer said for them for God's divine intervention to be felt by those needing the help and support from others.

Jesus' apostles understood from the example Jesus set while here on earth that we are here to love and serve each other, not ourselves. We are not to seek payment for everything we do to aid those around us. We are to humbly help as we are able, showing God's love to the least, the lost and the lonely. We are to help our neighbors as we would want to be helped in any given situation. It is by sharing God's love through our actions that His love is made complete in us and through us.

Prayer

Dearest Lord Jesus, help us to open our eyes to see what it is You would have us do to show Your love to others – especially to those in need of help or comfort. Amen.

BE PREPARED

Since we are God's offspring,
we ought not to think that the deity is like gold,
or silver, or stone,
an image formed by the art and imagination of mortals.
While God has overlooked the times of human ignorance,
now he commands all people everywhere to repent,
because he has fixed a day
on which he will have the world judged in righteousness
by a man whom he has appointed,
and of this he has given assurance to all
by raising him from the dead.'
~ Acts 17:29-31

We, as humans, often put things off for "another day," as if we have all the time in the world to worry about our mortality. Others pass away, but we seem to be unable to comprehend that we will not always be here. We often feel that "just one more time" on this or that sinful activity and I will stop, but will we really be able to stop and repent in time?

God has set forth a day and time that He will judge the world through His Son. Not even Jesus knows the time or day, but it is coming. All of the calamities and wars around us are but a few small signs that the time is coming soon!

We must stop putting off our repentance to God and give up what is sinful in our lives now. We cannot put it off any longer. We must start examining where we need to change and start living a life worthy of Christ – giving love and help to those who are the least, the lost and the last in society today. We must help bring His love to others so we all can be prepared to stand before Christ on that day not to far in the future and be able to be judged as worthy of His redemption and eternal life.

Are you prepared? What do you need to do to get on track with God? Have you given yourself over to Him to use as His servant in this world we live in? If not, it isn't too late!

Prayer

Dearest Father in Heaven, we thank You that it is still not too late to ask for your forgiveness for all of the sinful ways that still cling to us. Wash us clean from this sinful nature and place in our hearts the desire to serve You as You wish to use us to further Your kingdom by preparing ourselves and others for Your day of judgment. Amen.

No Complaints

And do not complain as some of them did,
and were destroyed by the destroyer.
These things happened to them to serve as an example,
and they were written down to instruct us,
on whom the ends of the ages have come.
So if you think you are standing,
watch out that you do not fall.
No testing has overtaken you
that is not common to everyone.
God is faithful,
and he will not let you be tested beyond your strength,
but with the testing he will also provide the way out
so that you may be able to endure it.
~ 1 Corinthians 10:10-13

It was "National No Complaint Day." So many of us complain about so many trifles throughout the day that we often don't realize we are doing it. What if we could go without complaining for just one day? How would our day be impacted by only looking at the positive side of life?

Complaining often leaves us unhappy in our situations and life itself. The Bible says that we should not complain as others do. What we are going through or feeling is never more than we and God together can't handle. We need to look for the positive side of the situation for our lives to be happier and more fulfilling.

Sure, someone has a bigger and better-looking home than you, but they also have bigger mortgage payments, higher upkeep costs, higher taxes, and on and on. Be happy with what God has given you. In your contentment, you will find greater satisfaction than worrying about what you do not have.

Someone has better health than you? Perhaps they won't see and appreciate the love of God shining through the care of others toward them this day as you do. True, good health is a wonderful thing, but so many of us take good health for granted and tend to not look for God's love being shown to us when all is going well.

In all things, look for the silver lining of God's love and care for you. He will never test you beyond what you can handle with Him at your side, nor will He forget you. This wonderful, all-encompassing love from Him is something we should always rejoice about in all situations of life instead of looking at the negatives. We have nothing to complain about when we know that God does all things for good to come to us.

Prayer

Heavenly Father, so often we complain about the most trivial things in our lives. Help us to concentrate on the positives in our lives and not the negatives, as You will always give us what is good for us, as a loving parent cares for their child. Amen.

Show Me the Path

Make me to know your ways, O Lord;
teach me your paths.
Lead me in your truth, and teach me,
for you are the God of my salvation;
for you I wait all day long.
*~ **Psalm 25:4-5***

A parishioner came in to borrow some tables and chairs. As he re-entered the office, he asked me if I was housing a beaver in the bush outside. I looked at him very puzzled, but he had me follow him out to the vestibule. I went between the two sets of entrance doors to have a look at the outside bushes and he quietly told me that I was looking in the wrong direction. He then motioned to the artificial plant between two small pew-like chairs in the vestibule. There, hiding behind the plant base was a ground hog! He was frightened and hoping we would not harm him.

The parishioner told me he could get him out for me, so I propped open both exterior doors and he ever so gently prodded the groundhog out from behind the plant with a broom. The groundhog raced over to the other side of the vestibule and stood up with his front paws on the glass looking to the outside as he franticly looked for a way out, not realizing that he had just run by the two open doors leading him out to safety. Again, the parishioner gently prodded him and he raced up to one of the two open doors, stood up on his hind legs again with his front paws on the glass, looking at the bushes outside, not realizing that he needed only move to his left for freedom. Finally, after one more gentle prod, he saw the direction he needed to go and he raced down the sidewalk to freedom. We often get ourselves on the wrong paths in life and need God's gentle nudging to lead us back on the right path. Through quiet meditation to commune with God and through reading His Word, the Holy Bible, we can find the direction that God wants us to take. We don't always get our directions straight the first time we try to find our way back to Him, but He will keep nudging us gently in the right direction until we find His pathway once again that leads to a closer relationship with Him.

Stay focused on God. Listen for His direction when you are lost on the wrong path of life. God will guide you back to Him. Just stay open to His touch as He gently nudges you back to the safety of His love and shelter.

Prayer

Dear Lord, thank you for always watching over us, willing to guide us back to the safety of Your loving arms when we stray off of Your path. Help us to always be ready to detect Your gentle touch leading us back onto the pathway that leads to You. Amen.

SPREAD THE WORD
COMMUNICATING IN TODAY'S WORLD

*What I say to you in the dark, tell in the light;
and what you hear whispered, proclaim from the housetops.*
~ ***Matthew 10:27***

I am part of an amazing group of people within my church family that shares different aspects of communications of events within our church and throughout our community. We are gaining more and more avenues with which to communicate with today's technology available to us. We have the internet website, e-mail, twitter, online newspaper blogs, radio, telephone, TV, regular newspapers, flyers, newsletters, AV screens during worship, etc. To coordinate our efforts, we each are assigned different avenues in which to communicate news and events given to our committee for publication.

Back in Jesus' time, they had word of mouth for the most part, as written forms of communication were not common like today. People that heard Jesus' message were to proclaim it via word of mouth to all who would hear. Not everyone was willing to listen, though. Some hearers became violent and ran Jesus' followers out of town or even stoned them later on, after Jesus' death and resurrection.

Our task in today's society is to use what is available to us to further the Good News of Jesus Christ. It isn't just for a committee or a pastor to do. We all are called to share the love of Christ – in person or via the many new avenues of communication available to us today.

What message of Christ's love do you have to share with others? How will you spread the Good News today and every day to bring others into the light of Christ's love? It is time to "shout it from the rooftops," so let's start communicating in the name of Jesus Christ!

Prayer

Dear Blessed Savior, thank you for Your constant love for us and for the saving grace which You have made available to all who will listen and believe in You. Help us to make the time to share this Good News with others to bring them into the light of Your love. Amen.

SPREAD THE WORD
TAKING WHAT HAS BEEN STARTED
AND MOVING IT FORWARD

But thanks be to God,
who in Christ always leads us in triumphal procession,
and through us spreads in every place
the fragrance that comes from knowing him.
~ 2 Corinthians 2:14

Our Men's Ministry group received a truckload of sweet corn from a local farmer who donates some of his produce for distribution to local food pantries. Our men then came to our parking lot, where this bounty has been dropped off to move it out to the local pantries. There was always more than what they could handle or distribute, so they, in turn, called other local churches to also come and take what they needed to distribute to people in their areas that were in need as well.

When we hear the Good News that Jesus Christ has to offer us, we are not to hoard it for ourselves. Jesus' message is sufficient to save all those who will hear and accept His saving grace. Jesus has a limitless supply to give to all, not just a few select people to benefit from His sacrifice so many years ago. It is up to us, those that have received this grace and forgiveness to continue spreading the Word of salvation to those that have not yet heard or accepted this gift freely given to all.

How can you spread the Word today? Who around you has not yet heard about or accepted this great gift of love and mercy? Open your eyes to see where you can further His kingdom around you.

Prayer

Lord, use me to spread Your Word to all who will hear! Amen.

Nowhere to Hide ~ God's Light Exposes All

'For his eyes are upon the ways of mortals,
and he sees all their steps.

There is no gloom or deep darkness
where evildoers may hide themselves.
*~ **Job 34:21-22***

From the window above and across the narrow drive in back of the church, the early morning light revealed a spider strand sparkling in sunlight here and there when the leaves parted enough to allow the sun to shed its light on them. If I were to just wander down through the path to the little stream bed within, I would more than likely not notice the spider's silvery strands until they were already clinging to me with their stickiness that helps the spider catch its prey.

Sin is a lot like a spider strand. We don't always notice it until it has "clung" to us - trapping us like Satan's prey. We remain trapped in this stickiness of sin until being able to wipe ourselves clean through repentant prayer when God's light has revealed to us what we have "sticking to us."

Let us be more aware of what we are "walking into" each day. Try to see the "spider strands" of sin for what they are BEFORE walking into them. Perhaps, if we are more vigilant to our surroundings, we will be less likely to get ourselves into the "sticky situations" that Satan has lying in wait to trap us with.

Prayer

Dear Lord, always have Your Light shining brightly for us to see the sinful traps that lie in wait for us to get stuck in. Help us to be able to "walk around" and avoid these things so that our path is always a clear, clean walk toward You. Amen.

Attention! Attention!
What Does God Have to Do
to Get Your Attention?

'If they will not believe you or heed the first sign,
they may believe the second sign.
If they will not believe even these two signs or heed you,
you shall take some water from the Nile
and pour it on the dry ground;
and the water that you shall take from the Nile
will become blood on the dry ground.'
~ Exodus 4:8-9

We often get caught up in our own lives and forget that God is beside us at all times - through the good times and the bad. We have a habit of calling on Him when we need help for things out of our control, but how often do we connect with God when things are going right in our lives? God wants our attention at all times. He wants to share the joys and the sorrows of life with us, not just the difficulties of our lives.

The Egyptians long ago failed to pay attention to the signs God was showing them to let His people have their freedom and allow them to return to their own land. They suffered many plagues - each one worse than the next until finally the death of the first born in all households in Egypt got their attention enough to allow the Jewish people to be set free.

Are we willing to give God the attention He would like to have from us? Are we willing to praise Him for all of the wonderful things He has given us in our lives as well as for the difficulties that tend to get us to give Him our attention? Are we able to learn to give God our undivided attention to listen to what He wants us to do with our lives in His name?

We must open our ears to hear Him calling us, and then reply, "Yes, Lord. I hear You. Tell me what Your will is for me today." Then go out and complete the task He is calling us to accomplish for Him to bring glory to His Name.

Prayer

Father in Heaven, we often go about our days so wrapped up in ourselves and what WE feel is important instead of listening to You with our undivided attention. Help us to seek Your will in our lives and to share all aspects of our lives with You - giving You the glory in good times and in bad. Amen.

Seek Him
Looking for Signs of God With Us

'And you, my son Solomon, know the God of your father,
and serve him with single mind and willing heart;
for the Lord searches every mind,
and understands every plan and thought.
If you seek him, he will be found by you;
but if you forsake him, he will abandon you for ever.'
~ 1 Chronicles 28:9

Looking out the window of the upper floor of the church one morning, I was able to view the lush green of the last days of summer hiding the small stream bed within it. The sun tried to pierce the shadows of the early morning with small glimpses of light between the swaying of the branches overhead. As I focused more closely, I was able to spy the movement of the little lives that call this place "home." One squirrel made a made dash up the other side of the stream bed. Another hopped from branch to branch in the tree above. Then, in the tall weeds right next to the drive, I noticed another pop his head above the growth while he quickly ate some small morsel he had discovered for his morning meal.

If we take the time to stop rushing about in our busy lives and look for signs of God with us, we WILL find them. They can be as subtle as the smile from a young child or as bold as a miracle of healing. When we really take the time to look for Him, we will find that He has always been right beside us, waiting for us to give Him our attention, but if we abandon Him, He will abandon us in the Day of Judgment.

Seek God daily in all things - good and bad - and thank Him for always being there to lead you through this earthly life you were given. Your faithfulness to Him will be rewarded in the end of time for all eternity. Will you be found to be one of the faithful, or one that abandoned Him? The choice is yours to make.

Prayer

Loving God, we thank you for Your eternal presence beside us in all aspects of our lives. Help us to recognize Your hand in our lives and the lives of those around us and to remain faithful to You all the days of our lives. Amen.

LET US GO TO THE HOUSE OF GOD

and many nations shall come and say:
'Come, let us go up to the mountain of the Lord,
to the house of the God of Jacob;
that he may teach us his ways
and that we may walk in his paths.'
For out of Zion shall go forth instruction,
and the word of the Lord from Jerusalem.
*~ **Micah 4:2***

Fall was coming quickly. I love this season, with its array of colors popping out of the formerly green landscape. My most favorite time is when the wind knocks a large quantity of leaves off of the tree during the night and I am one of the first to drive the path from the street, up the hill to work. If the path is completely covered in leaves, it seems to quiet the noise of my drive to an almost silent approach through this beautiful park-like setting. It makes coming to work such a peaceful thing.

The fact that my work is located at my church makes the above passage even a bit more meaningful to me. Not only am I going to work, but I am going to the house of God! Sunday is not the only day to learn His ways. Throughout any given day, of which no two are exactly the same, I have the opportunity to experience God in His home on a daily basis throughout the week. I see people needing comfort and prayer as well as people coming in to celebrate joys in their lives with those of us that are at the church and willing to listen. We greet people with the love and hospitality of Jesus Christ every day. It is a very rare thing for me to leave the house of the Lord and feel totally spent through the work that was accomplished. Instead, I leave feeling happy and rejuvenated with doing my work to please Him.

So let us go to the house of God! Let us feel His love and compassion surrounding us as we seek to learn His direction in our life. He is ready to let you in. Are you ready for a visit with Him?

Prayer

Dear Father in Heaven, thank You for letting us visit You in Your house of worship, not only on Sunday, but also throughout the week. We thank you for the opportunities to learn more about Your path and how to live our lives for Your glory. May we always feel renewed by our visits with You - both in Your house of worship and throughout our daily walks with You by our side. Amen.

REJOICE!

Yours, O Lord, are the greatness, the power,
the glory, the victory, and the majesty;
for all that is in the heavens and on the earth is yours;
yours is the kingdom, O Lord,
and you are exalted as head above all.
Riches and honor come from you, and you rule over all.
In your hand are power and might;
and it is in your hand to make great
and to give strength to all.
And now, our God, we give thanks to you
and praise your glorious name.
~ 1 Chronicles 29:11-13

Each day the colors of fall became more and more vibrant. As I drove to work, I marveled at the beauty of the trees as they changed from green to reds, yellows, burgundies and browns. What a wonderful thing to be able to rejoice in the changing of seasons when we look with awe at the power of God's hand in His creation.

Change within our lives can be a scary thing, yet we need to embrace and rejoice in it as well. It may be in one's health, status or relationships. With change, however "scary" it may be, God is present with us to make of the change something beautiful to behold. We must just place our trust in Him - that His plan is far better and greater than we can see or even imagine.

Change is not always something we look forward to, however. With God beside us, it will come to be something wonderful at then end of the journey. Just look to Him and believe.

Prayer

Heavenly Father, not all change is something we, as mere humans, enjoy going through. It can be very scary for us, yet exciting at other times. We place our faith and trust in You, that You know what is best for us, will continue to be with us and will see us through whatever changes in life we must go through. May we always remember that what You have in store for us is far better and more beautiful than we can even imagine and that we need to rejoice in the changes You have planned for us. Amen.

GIVING VS. RECEIVING

'Ask, and it will be given to you; search, and you will find;
knock, and the door will be opened for you.
For everyone who asks receives,
and everyone who searches finds,
and for everyone who knocks, the door will be opened.
Is there anyone among you who,
if your child asks for bread, will give a stone?
Or if the child asks for a fish, will give a snake?
If you then, who are evil,
know how to give good gifts to your children,
how much more will your Father in heaven give good things
to those who ask him!
*~ **Matthew 7:7-11***

Having had only one daughter out of my two children, she has laid claim to any jewelry I might hand down the line one day. In particular, this claim was to a ring I had had handed down to me by my grandmother, who had passed away at the young age of 53 due to cancer. The stones were part of my grandmother's mother's wedding set - one fourth of the diamonds and sapphires went to each of the three daughters and one daughter-in-law and placed into a setting of their choice. My daughter didn't expect it to go to her for many years yet, but as a special gift to her for a very big moment in her life I decided no greater gift could I find to mark this particular occasion and milestone. I wanted to see her enjoy it as much as I had for the many years I wore it, remembering my grandmother that had passed away so young in life, yet had always made a point of showing her love to me when we were together.

My mother, in seeing this event unfold, proceeded to hand down her original wedding set that had been reset into one ring 30 years ago to me for my birthday (not having realized I had just become the age at which her mother passed away). I had no idea this was coming, but was overwhelmed by the love with which it was given to me. In addition to the ring, it was given to me in a special little jewelry box with my name on the heart-shaped key charm that decorates the lock on the front of the box. This particular box was chosen by my father. He insisted that my first and middle name be on the charm when they purchased it. This additional touch made the gift even more meaningful to me - that not only was my mother handing down to me their symbol of love, but that they were personalizing it specifically for me.

God sent us the greatest gift of all - His one and only Son - to bring us all back into a relationship with Him. The love and sacrifice Jesus was sent to give to us and demonstrate to all around Him is what we are to emulate and pass on as a heritage in our lifetime to others. Christmas is the season of gift giving, but the greatest gift we have to offer one another - both family and stranger to us - is the love and service we have to offer in the name of Jesus Christ. Not only does giving this most amazing gift to others warm our hearts, but we receive the approval from our Heavenly Father for these gifts given in the name of His Son. Let the celebration begin today and continue year round to share our love and service with everyone we encounter!

Prayer

Dearest Heavenly Father, we thank you for your greatest gift of love and sacrifice all wrapped up in Your Son, Jesus Christ. May we emulate Your greatest gift by sharing this gift with others all year round in the name of Your Son - handing down this heirloom of love and service to all we encounter. Amen.

LIFE IS WONDERFUL!

We who are strong
ought to put up with the failings of the weak,
and not to please ourselves.
Each of us must please our neighbor
for the good purpose of building up the neighbor.
For Christ did not please himself; but, as it is written,
'The insults of those who insult you have fallen on me.'
~ ***Romans 15:1-3***

As Christmas drew nearer, I saw many classic movies showing up on the television. The one that really brought home a message to me is *"It's a Wonderful Life."* The message of hope when things seem their very darkest was brought to life through the characters as the story unfolded. When George felt he was worth more dead than alive, Clarence, his guardian angel, showed him just how much of a difference he had made to those around him and how life would be so much the worse for others if George had never been born.

Everyone has those moments when they wonder why they were even put on this earth. Just what kind of difference do they make anyway? People don't always realize their importance in the lives of those around them. Even though we must remain humble in the service to our Lord, we must also try to remember that we are important. We DO matter to those around us. We are a very important part of God's plan for this world. This life we have been given is very wonderful indeed!

Prayer

Heavenly Father, when things seem to feel so heavy and burdensome to us, when we are feeling at our very lowest, help us to always remember that we are important to You and that no matter what, You love us through it all. Amen.

CHANGING OF THE "SEASONS"

yet he has not left himself without a witness in doing good—
giving you rains from heaven and fruitful seasons,
and filling you with food and your hearts with joy.'
~ Acts 14:17

The next day was to mark the season of spring, and with it we begin to notice that robins were returning to the area after a long, snowy, cold season of winter. The snows had melted away into the grounds that longed to turn green as temperatures began to rise. Rains returned to us as the bulbs erupted through the brown ground cover that had helped insulate them from the cold of the season before.

Like seasons, people in our lives come and go as well. While they are with us, our relationships grow stronger, like a bulb coming forth from the grounds in springtime. We bask in the warmth of their friendship and love, as does the flower in summer. As they move on to other places over time, we feel a loss like the trees losing their leaves in the fall as we remember the good times we shared. Then the empty space in our lives is like the cold, barrenness of winter as we miss those that have moved on. Even during these lonely times of life, we must remember that the next spring season is just around the corner. New people will come into our lives to once again grow new, strong relationships. This cycle continues throughout our lives.

Let us not dwell on the "falls" and "winters" of our lives, for each season brings with it something good from our Heavenly Father. Although people come and go throughout our lifetime, God provides for us the relationships we need at the times we need them. We must just be open to allowing the "shoots" of spring to grow into the strong plants of new relationships in another season of our life when He provides them. Keep looking for where God is trying to grow relationships around you and use these opportunities to draw nearer to God and to help bring the new "shoots" of friendship with you in His divine presence as well.

Prayer

Lord, as our seasons of life cycle by, one after the other, may we always be open to seeing the newness of life and relationships that you provide us throughout our lives. Help us to cultivate strong friendships and help us draw ourselves, and those around us closer to You. Amen.

FEELING GOD ALL AROUND YOU

As a mother comforts her child,
so I will comfort you;
you shall be comforted in Jerusalem.
~ Isaiah 66:13

Have you ever felt God all around you? Have you ever stopped to look for Him? Everyday senses that we feel may actually be God's presence all around us.

Peering out the window this morning, I was struck by the thought that every time the breeze blows across my face, I may actually be having my face caressed by the hand of God, much like a mother will gently caress the face of her child. When the sun breaks through the cloudy day to warm me from the coolness of the day, this could actually be God enfolding me with the warm embrace of His love. When the rain drops fall upon me, this may either be God cleansing me from the dirtiness of society around me as a mother gently washes the face of her child with sticky hints of treats on their face or sharing tears of joy or sorrow that I may be feeling at the time. God is not some far-off deity that awaits our moments of need to visit with Him. He is always here among us – sharing our every moment as a loving parent watches over a young toddler. His very presence shows us just how much He desires to be a part of our lives throughout our day – not just when we are in trouble and need His help.

Take some time to feel His presence with you today. When you feel that next little breeze across your cheek, imagine God's loving hand caressing your face as He whispers quietly in your ear, "I love you." Then feel your heart fill with the knowledge that He is always with you, wanting the very best for you, just as a loving parent wishes for their child.

Prayer

Dearest Heavenly Father, thank you for always letting us feel your presence with us if we just stop to sense it. Help us to always take time to see you with us in our everyday life – guiding us and showing us Your love in so many ways. Amen.

NEW BEGINNINGS

Blessed be the God and Father of our Lord Jesus Christ!
By his great mercy he has given us a new birth
into a living hope
through the resurrection of Jesus Christ from the dead,
and into an inheritance that is imperishable,
undefiled, and unfading, kept in heaven for you,
who are being protected by the power of God
through faith for a salvation
ready to be revealed in the last time.
~ 1 Peter 1:3-5

May and June usually are the times we see many young people graduating from school. Whether it is from pre-school, junior high, senior high, college or graduate school, each graduation not only marks the end to a student's accomplishments, but also a new beginning. They may be moving on to a different school for further education or out on their own into the working world to put what they have learned to good use. Whatever the case, they all mark a time of new beginnings.

Each day can also herald a new beginning for anyone coming to Christ. They repent of their old ways and take on the beginnings of living their new life in Christ. Taking this new-found faith in their Lord and Savior helps them to see the world in a new way as they look for ways to serve Him in their community and around the world.

Each person has a gift that God has bestowed upon them to carry out Christ's mission here on earth. Once they find this gift within themselves, it opens up a whole new life for them as they become the light of Christ leading others to the love and knowledge of redeeming grace through Jesus. New beginnings for them and for others are a never-ending chain of events.

How can you help bring a new beginning into someone's life? What gift has God bestowed upon you to use to further His kingdom here on earth? Today is a new beginning for you to search within yourself to find that gift and lead others to their new beginning of a life with Christ.

Prayer

Lord of new beginnings, help me seek the gift You have given me to use in the name of Christ to further Your kingdom by leading others to You. Amen.

RENEW, RE-ENERGIZE AND RESTORE

The LORD is my chosen portion and my cup;
you hold my lot.
The boundary lines have fallen for me in pleasant places;
I have a goodly heritage.

I bless the LORD who gives me counsel;
in the night also my heart instructs me.
I keep the LORD always before me;
because he is at my right hand, I shall not be moved.

Therefore my heart is glad, and my soul rejoices;
my body also rests secure.
*~ **Psalm 16:5-9***

The ending of the school year heralds vacation season for many. This long-awaited time of year is a time to renew, re-energize and restore ourselves before returning to work or another year of school. We look forward to good weather, relaxing, traveling, or catching up with family and friends.

Whether we are at work, school or rest, God is always there for us. We rest in the knowledge that we are safe in His loving presence wherever we may be. Does this mean that all around us will be "sunshine, lollypops and rainbows"? No, of course not. However, no matter what might befall us here, we have the eternal hope of our Lord with us through it all. In good times and in bad, we can rest secure – knowing that God will keep us safe from the eternal evils that surround us here in this life and that one day we will be with Him in all of His eternal glory to worship and adore in person.

May you find the time to rest from the daily struggles of this life by setting aside some time to visit with God for some treasured "one-on-one" time to renew, re-energize and restore you by strengthening your relationship with Him. Concentrate on only the positives and see just how much He really loves you. Enjoy a day in His creation – marveling at all He has created for you to enjoy. Then, at the end of the day, thank God for all of the many blessings He has given you personally. You are a treasured child of God!

Prayer

Dear Father in Heaven, I thank you for all of the many blessings You have given me – no matter how big or small they may be. I thank you for Your endless love that surrounds and protects me throughout my life and for the knowledge that one day I will see you face to face to worship for all eternity. Amen.

Welcoming the Stranger

Let mutual love continue.
Do not neglect to show hospitality to strangers,
for by doing that
some have entertained angels without knowing it.
~ Hebrews 13:1-2

Many of us tend to shy away from people we do not know, yet most of us have had experiences of chatting briefly in the check-out line at a store with someone who is a stranger to us. We see strangers enter our church and, instead of welcoming them, we tend to continue to speak to only those we already know. Many times, these strangers in our lives pass by never to be seen again, but God has a purpose for everything. What was the purpose of their presence in our lives at that moment that we may have missed?

Some strangers are placed in our daily lives for us to show the love of God to. They may not have a relationship with God and are in the process of seeking out His very presence to fill that void in their lives. It is our job to be there to help show them the way to a meaningful life with Jesus as their Savior. Sometimes, that stranger you are encountering is on the brink of a very dark place in their life and your kindness to them may be just the thing they need to see that there are better times ahead for them. We can be their "angel" from God to bring them back to the life God wants them to live.

Some strangers are placed into our daily routines to help remind us of God's love for us. Our day may not be going as well as we would like, but that welcoming smile or kind word of a stranger may be just the thing to help turn our day around.

They can be the "angels" God has sent to us to remind us that He cares about us and that He has not left us alone to deal with our troubles by ourselves.

What can you do today to show hospitality to a stranger? How can you be an "angel" to someone you do not know? Maybe you can "pay it forward" at the fast food drive-up window by paying for the meal behind you. Make it a point to speak to the stranger that enters your church this Sunday or is in the check-out line with you. You may not only be their "angel", but perhaps they may be your "angel" as well.

Prayer

Heavenly Father, help me to be Your "angel" to those I do not know, and may I recognize the "angels" You send to be in my life for those short moments You are reminding me that You are with me always. Amen.

How Will You Be Remembered?

For we know, brothers and sisters beloved by God,
that he has chosen you,
because our message of the gospel
came to you not in word only,
but also in power and in the Holy Spirit
and with full conviction;
just as you know what kind of people we proved to be
among you for your sake.
And you became imitators of us and of the Lord,
for in spite of persecution
you received the word with joy inspired by the Holy Spirit,
so that you became an example to all the believers…
~ 1 Thessalonians 1:4-7a

While going through my great-grandmother's scrapbook of her many memories throughout her life, I was drawn to the colorful reporting by the newspaper articles she had saved – especially how the obituaries were worded. Some of her friends and relatives were very active in their church and recounted in detail how they had served in many various capacities within their church and their communities as they served others to "promote the good of the cause." This cause was spreading the love and message of Jesus Christ to bring others into fellowship with Him.

We, as Christians, are all called to this very purpose – to serve others and be examples of Jesus Christ in the world around us today. By being examples of His love and care for others, we may draw those not yet in a relationship with Him to a new life in Christ. We must also remember that it is not our work, but our allowing the work of the Holy Spirit within us to be a transforming force to the world in which we now live. By allowing the Holy Spirit to work within us, we may also be remembered for the love and service we were able to share as vessels of God's ultimate plan while we were allowed to remain here in this life.

We must ask ourselves how we can serve within our church, community and the world around us. Every one of us has a God-given gift provided to us by the Holy Spirit. We can do all types of tasks to carry the message and love of Christ to all "corners" of the world today. Tasks as simple as extending a word of care in the form of a card or letter to those in prison or who are ailing, to as self-less and labor-intensive as becoming a missionary in a foreign land can be performed by those to whom the Holy Spirit fills with the ability to achieve these acts of love in the name of Christ. Once we find the task that we are being called to do, we must act to carry out the task as long as God allows us the ability during our lifetime by allowing the Holy Spirit to work within us.

Prayer

Father in Heaven, we thank you for the Holy Spirit that you have given to us to enable us to serve You with the gifts You have blessed us with. May we always strive to serve You with these gifts by allowing Your Spirit to work within us and through us to bring Your love and message to all. May our service for You be what is remembered about us once we leave this world to join You in Your heavenly kingdom. Amen.

HINDSIGHT

And he said, 'I will make all my goodness pass before you,
and will proclaim before you the name,
"The Lord";and I will be gracious
to whom I will be gracious,
and will show mercy on whom I will show mercy.
But', he said, 'you cannot see my face;
for no one shall see me and live.'
And the Lord continued,
'See, there is a place by me
where you shall stand on the rock;
and while my glory passes by
I will put you in a cleft of the rock,
and I will cover you with my hand until I have passed by;
then I will take away my hand, and you shall see my back;
but my face shall not be seen.'
*~ **Exodus 33:19-23***

The bright morning sunshine pours into the east window of our church fellowship area when I first arrive at workon sunny days. As I try to look out into the trees of the ravine between the church and the cemetery, I find it very difficult to discern what is actually out there due to the glare of the sun. Later in the day, however, as the sun rises more into the mid-day sky, the glare is gone and I am able to make out what is actually there in the ravine as I wait for my coffee cup to fill at the single-serve machine.

God's presence among us can be very much like the brilliance of the morning sunshine that keeps us from seeing what is actually near us all along. God is always with us, but when we are going through difficult times, we do not always see Him walking beside us through the whole ordeal. It is only after we have reached the other side of the crisis that we can look back and actually see where God was at work in and around us through it all.

Are you or someone you know going through a difficult struggle? Do you see God working in subtle ways as you or they are walking through their difficult times? Keep looking! God IS always there through it all – sometimes, hind sight is better than present sight or foresight.

Prayer

Dearest Heavenly Father, thank you for never letting us walk alone through the many difficulties of this life we live on earth. Help us to always feel Your presence with us and around us - reminding us that we are never alone in this world and its many problems. You are our loving Father that always keeps His watchful eye on His children. Amen.

Pulling Up to the Line

For it is to your credit if, being aware of God,
you endure pain while suffering unjustly.
If you endure when you are beaten for doing wrong,
where is the credit in that?
But if you endure when you do right and suffer for it,
you have God's approval.
For to this you have been called,
because Christ also suffered for you,
leaving you an example,
so that you should follow in his steps.
'He committed no sin, and no deceit was found in his mouth.'
When he was abused, he did not return abuse;
when he suffered, he did not threaten;
but he entrusted himself to the one who judges justly.
He himself bore our sins in his body on the cross,
so that, free from sins, we might live for righteousness;
by his wounds you have been healed.
For you were going astray like sheep,
but now you have returned to the shepherd
and guardian of your souls.
*~ **1 Peter 2:19-25***

As I pulled up to the red light on my way to work, I noticed that the car beside me stayed over a half car length back from the stop line instead of pulling all of the way up. I have noticed this other times recently as well. I am always puzzled by this, as to why they stay so far back – sometimes so far back that they do not trigger the light for their lane (if it is a turn lane). It caused me to ponder how this relates to our faith life in today's society.

So many people believe in God, yet they don't fully commit themselves to Him (much like stopping for the red light, but not pulling up to the stop line in traffic). God has that "line" where, when we truly believe in Him and give ourselves over to Him and His will, we are showing our faith that He will use us for what He created us to be and to complete while here on earth instead of stubbornly holding back to "do our own thing" while claiming that we have faith in Him.

How are you "holding back" in your faith in God? What can you do to "pull up" to His "stop line" and allow God to "take the wheel of your life" to use you for His will in this world? Take your "foot off of the brake" and roll on up to God's "stop line", stopping your willfulness and allowing your faith in Him to take you farther than you ever imagined in this life so as to claim your eternal reward when the "light turns green" and you travel on past this life to your eternal reward.

Prayer

Lord, I know I am stubborn and hold back to do my own selfish things in this world. Help me to "pull up" to your "stop line" and allow You to take over the wheel of my life to accomplish all you have put me in this world to do in Your name instead of wasting my time doing what "I" want to do. Amen.

PAST AND PRESENT LEAD TO THE FUTURE

I remember the days of old,
I think about all your deeds,
I meditate on the works of your hands.
~ Psalm 143:5

As I looked out the window one morning, I noticed how gloomy the sky looked, with the gray clouds hiding the sunlight from an otherwise beautiful fall morning. The trees along the creek bed were slowly changing to their beautiful warm colors of red and gold as the small glimmer of water could be seen winding its way down the slight incline running beside the church I work in. The contrast of gloom and beautiful colors is much like life – some parts of our lives are better than others with joys and sorrows intermixed to make us who we are today.

I start to wonder again what the church grounds used to look like before the church was built here. This was a former church camp that thrived during the summer with revivals that lasted a week or two at a time. Thousands of people would come in horse and buggy to camp here and listen to the Word of God and renew their spirit on these very grounds that still are filled with the trees that witnessed many coming to Christ.

Past and present events in our lives can help us see what direction God is telling us to go in our lives for the future. Seeing what we have experienced in the past, we can better understand how to help others along life's journey in finding God in their own lives. Seeing God working in the lives of those around us now can help inspire us to continue living our own lives in service to God at new levels and in new ways.

Meditating on God and His many works in this world is a great way to map out our future – living our life for Christ.

Prayer

Dear Lord, thank you for the memories, both good and bad, that have molded us into the persons we are today. Help us to use these past experiences to serve others in a way that leads others to You and Your loving embrace. Amen.

In the Likeness of God

So God created humankind in his image,
in the image of God he created them;
male and female he created them.
*~ **Genesis 1:27***

Looking at a post on my computer one morning, I was drawn to an image of beautiful birds – one of each color of the rainbow. Below this image was a group of children – one from each ethnicity here on earth. Below this image was a message asking why we can appreciate the beauty of creation in all that is around us, yet we do not appreciate the differences in each other. This really got to me. I have a very blended extended family, so I don't think much about the differences between ethnicities. The media, on the other hand, seems to really enjoy publicizing our differences in a most negative way, churning up bitterness between the races.

Recently, a sister in Christ of mine and I compared notes on this very subject. She, being of a different ethnicity than I, said she always envied the hair my ethnicity, while I expressed how I loved the many shades of skin tones and complexions of hers. Why doesn't the media see the positives instead of the negatives as we do? God did create us all in His likeness. He did not express that one ethnicity was better than the other. He did chose a people to claim as His own, yet He gave His only Son to us through his chosen people to bring us all back in relationship to Him.

I think if the media would quit giving so much attention to the negatives between peoples and instead concentrate on the positives between us, hate would not continue to grow for each other at such an alarming rate. Instead, those that are wary of other ethnicities might actually see others different from themselves in looks as being just as beautiful as they are in the sight of God and perhaps help change their hearts for the better toward one another.

How can we help bring others different than ourselves to a closer relationship with one another and to Christ? How can we, as God's people, learn to put aside any biases we have and chose to love each other as Christ loves us? We need to learn to put blinders on when it comes to seeing others differently and instead, look for our positive commonalities to create the loving family of God here on earth.

Prayer

Dear Lord, it is so disturbing to see all of the negativity and hate in this world. Help us to see others as you see us – as your beautiful creation that is to come together as one to worship You as brothers and sisters who all share you as Our Father. Amen.

Let Your Faith Dance in Praise!

Praise the Lord!
Praise God in his sanctuary;
praise him in his mighty firmament!
Praise him for his mighty deeds;
praise him according to his surpassing greatness!

Praise him with trumpet sound;
praise him with lute and harp!
Praise him with tambourine and dance;
praise him with strings and pipe!
Praise him with clanging cymbals;
praise him with loud clashing cymbals!
Let everything that breathes praise the Lord!
Praise the Lord!
~ Psalm 150

Fall had finally arrived. The multi-colored leaves had begun to fall and scuttled across the ground. A swift breeze swirled a group of leaves into a circular whirlwind, allowing them to perform their final dance of autumn across the parking lot while the sun's spotlight illuminated their short-lived, graceful movements before me.

We can learn from these leaves. In our lives, we need to make sure that we "dance in praise" to our Heavenly Father for all He has given us! Yes, there are days we really don't feel like lifting our hearts in praise ~ especially when life seems to be dragging us down. Yet even the leaves of fall dance in praise when life has "brought them down" from their better days of life attached to their trees. Just because life isn't always being lived on a "high note" doesn't mean there isn't something to be grateful for and able to lift up in praise to God. Maybe our health is failing, maybe we can't get around like we used to, but we can always give praise to God for yet another day in which to share in the love of friends and family, a roof over our heads, the ability to experience the beauty of each day He has allowed us to see or for the food He has provided for us.

You say you can't dance? Well, maybe your dance doesn't have to be a physical dance, but rather allowing your heart to and soul move to the beat of a silent "music" of faith within your own being can be your dance of faith. However you choose to dance, let yourself go to the beat of life itself to praise God for all He has blessed you with.

Prayer

Dear Lord, thank you for yet another beautiful day to share in Your creation. Let my life dance in praise before You for all You have chosen to bless me with. Amen.

BEHOLD THE GOLD

And the twelve gates are twelve pearls,
each of the gates is a single pearl,
and the street of the city is pure gold,
transparent as glass.
*~ **Revelation 21:21***

With the season of fall comes the beautiful colors of the leaves. The reds, russets, yellows, browns and golds that I see herald in the end of the warm weather season and remind me that colder weather is just around the corner. Outside my window, I watch the changes in the ravine from the dense, dark greens to the changes of these warm palette colors our Heavenly Father paints for me to enjoy as the year slowly begins to wind down. The otherwise brown and green floor of the ravine have turned into a beautiful golden carpet that, when the sun hits it just right, invites the child in me to return to treasured memories of my youth when my brothers and I would rake the leaves into piles and jump into them, laughing and giggling until the pile was so spread out, we had to rake it up again to start all over.

Gold has been highly valued for centuries by all people. The more we have, the higher our financial status within the community we live in. In sports, winning the gold medal shows that an athlete is the best in his field. This metal is still highly valued, sought after, and even guarded against theft by armed guards.

In Revelation, John paints us a picture of what heaven looks like. It is so hard to imagine gold so pure that it is transparent, but knowing the beauty of crystal when light hits it helps us to imagine a gold-ish hue of crystal so beautiful that it takes our breath away! We will never know the reality of this beauty here on earth, but oh, what a foretaste to our imagination of what awaits us when God finally calls us home!

When we leave this world, our hope is that we will be found worthy of entering this great city called heaven. It is the highest reward we can ever attain, although it comes with a price. We must leave this world to gain it. Our ability to enter into this city one day was paid for by the blood of Jesus Christ, who has given us that wonderful bridge that crosses the great divide between this life and eternal life with our Heavenly Father. We all hope that, by living our lives for Christ, we will one day "behold the gold" upon our entry into this great city to worship God face to face. Until that day, we must guard our hearts and souls from the selfish desires of our earthly life and instead invest heavily in service as a thank offering to God with whatever gifts He has blessed us with to help grow His kingdom in the hearts of others while we are still here.

Prayer

Lord, we know that we can never "earn" a place in heaven, as the price has already been paid for by Your Son, Jesus Christ. May we instead remember to serve You with a grateful heart, guarding ourselves against the evil desires of this world, so that we can help bring others to worship You as well and one day all gather in Your city of purest gold. Amen.

Wrapped in the Warmth of God's Love

In that region there were shepherds living in the fields,
keeping watch over their flock by night.
Then an angel of the Lord stood before them,
and the glory of the Lord shone around them,
and they were terrified. But the angel said to them, '
Do not be afraid; for see—
I am bringing you good news of great joy for all the people:
to you is born this day in the city of David a Savior,
who is the Messiah, the Lord. This will be a sign for you:
you will find a child wrapped in bands of cloth
and lying in a manger.'
And suddenly there was with the angel
a multitude of the heavenly host,
praising God and saying,
'Glory to God in the highest heaven,
and on earth peace among those whom he favors!'
*~ **Luke 2:8-14***

To most people that live in the northern states, Christmas doesn't really seem like Christmas without snow. Many people detest snow, except for this particular time of year. They will say that it can snow Christmas Eve and melt right after Christmas Day. We all want to have that perfect "postcard" scene of Christmas as we celebrate Christ's birth.

One year, it seemed we would have an unusually warm Christmas up north. El Niño had brought with it the winds and temperatures that would bring plenty of warmth and rain, but no snow to set the tone for our carols of ***"I'm Dreaming of a White Christmas"*** and ***"Jingle Bells"***. How could we really get in the Christmas Spirit without snow?

The shepherds and wise men didn't have these worries as they celebrated the very first Christmas. It didn't matter if there was snow, rain or warm temperatures. What mattered was the feeling of being wrapped in the warmth of God's love as they witnessed God's greatest gift before their very eyes - wrapped in a blanket to keep him warm in his stable bed or in his mother's arms.

As we celebrate this unusually warm Christmas this year, remember that God is wrapping us in the warmth of His love as we remember and celebrate the birth of His Son. We can rejoice in knowing that no matter the weather outside, God's love for us is constant and unwavering. As we experience the warmth of the weather, we need to imagine this warmth as God's warm embrace enfolding each of us in His love and continue to enjoy the season, even if we don't have the snow as we sing "Let It Snow, Let It Snow, Let It Snow!"

Prayer

Heavenly Father, may we all feel Your loving embrace as we celebrate Your greatest gift to us – the birth of Our Savior, who is Christ our Lord. Amen.

TURN TO GOD

Turn to me and be gracious to me,
for I am lonely and afflicted.
Relieve the troubles of my heart,
and bring me out of my distress.
Consider my affliction and my trouble,
and forgive all my sins.

Consider how many are my foes,
and with what violent hatred they hate me.
O guard my life, and deliver me;
do not let me be put to shame, for I take refuge in you.
May integrity and uprightness preserve me,
for I wait for you.
~ Psalm 25:16-21

Life is not always easy. There are bumps and potholes along the road of life that we all must experience, but how we handle those times matters a great deal to God. He does not want us to think we have to travel this road alone. It is times such as these that He especially wants us to turn our focus away from ourselves and back to Him.

It is always easy to praise God when things are going well in our lives. We have a tendency to forget to thank Him for all of the wonderful things He has done for us and given us, or we thank Him out of a routine prayer and are really only going through the motions of thanksgiving. We get so caught up in our own lives that we tend to leave God in the "back seat" as we continue to live for ourselves.

Perhaps these "bumps" and "pot holes" in our road are reminders from God that He is still here with us and waiting for us to acknowledge Him. Perhaps these jolts in our everyday lives are here to help us remember to lean on Him and that it is really God that is in control – not us. Does God want us to go through difficult times? No. However, when we do experience hard times along life's road, we must remember to let Him take over the driving for a while as we rest in His "passenger seat."

Prayer

Dear Heavenly Father, we know that you want the best for us and that You don't want us to have to go through difficult times alone. Please, take our difficulties from us and let us allow You to carry our load while we rest beside You, in the comfort of Your love. Amen.

Always with Us

'...And remember, I am with you always,
to the end of the age.'
*~ **Matthew 28:20b***

Outside my window, spring struggled to break free of winter's icy grasp. The leafless trees and bare ground cried out for the sun's warmth upon them so that they could once again look full of life. The creatures awaited the cover of foliage to hide their activities from predators in the area.

Our lives are sometimes very much like this time of year. We yearn to break free of our burdens or be healed of our illnesses that plague us daily. We often feel lost and alone in the day-to-day activities in which we participate. It is for the love and peace of our Heavenly Father that we eagerly await a new sense of hope and healing in this broken world in which we live.

God has told us through the vision seen by John that He "is with us always, to the end of the age." What wonderful news this is to us to know that, even when the world sees us as being lost and alone, we really aren't. We are like the earth just before spring, when what looks to be brown and empty really has new life springing up in the form of the first bulbs breaking through the ground, although still slightly hidden by the fallen leaves of autumn. God is always beside us. We just have to look for the signs of His presence - be it a friend that happens to call, a smile from a stranger, or the prayers lifted up on behalf of our needs by others. Remember, God is with us always.

Prayer

Heavenly Father, thank you for never leaving us, for always being there for us, even in our darkest times. Help us to feel Your presence with us and around us always. Amen.

as it is written in the book of the words of the prophet Isaiah,
'The voice of one crying out in the wilderness:
"Prepare the way of the Lord, make his paths straight.
Every valley shall be filled,
and every mountain and hill shall be made low,
and the crooked shall be made straight,
and the rough ways made smooth;
and all flesh shall see the salvation of God." '
~ Luke 3:4-6

Outside the window, I had noticed the once barren ground of winter was quickly being dressed by the green growth of spring. I could still see some bare spots, where the rains continued to erode the uncovered soil, but even that would soon be overtaken by grass and vines as they continued to spread out in the warmth of the sun. Even the leaves were popping out of their buds to help dress the trees in their annual green finery.

Lives often have barren times – times of sadness, illness, loss and stress. They often feel like they are never ending to those experiencing them. Sometimes it feels as though one barren time piles right down upon another, like a mudslide in the torrential rainstorm. It is in those times of deepest despair that many give up all hope of being saved, yet those who know God have the hope that they are not abandoned in these dark times.

We must always remember to keep our hearts and minds open even in the hardest times of our lives to allow God to work within our darkness to bring us out into the light of

His unfailing love. Only He can take our twisted paths of difficulties and make them lead straight to His renewing grace. He will fill the emptiness in our lives with the beauty of all He has provided for us. All obstacles can be overcome when we lean on His unfailing strength that will help make the hard times of this life more bearable. It is in the difficulties of our lives that we often see God's hand at work, pulling us out of the darkness and mire and into the light of His love.

As God fills in the barrenness of winter with the green growth of spring, so too will He fill our difficult times with His love, strength and grace to see us through to better times ahead. The emptiness of our lives can once again be filled with the beauty of the life He has created for us to live if we leave ourselves open to receive it from Him. Like the barren ground, we must allow the seeds of His unending love blossom in the light of His grace.

Prayer

Lord of my salvation, help us to keep our hearts and minds open to Your never ending love for us. Thank you for always walking beside us – leading us through the hardest times of our lives into the light of Your unending grace. Amen.

SIN: THE "BLACK MOLD" OF OUR LIVES

If your hand causes you to stumble, cut it off;
it is better for you to enter life maimed
than to have two hands and to go to hell,
to the unquenchable fire.
And if your foot causes you to stumble, cut it off;
it is better for you to enter life lame than to have two feet
and to be thrown into hell.
And if your eye causes you to stumble, tear it out;
it is better for you to enter the kingdom of God with one eye
than to have two eyes
and to be thrown into hell, where their worm never dies,
and the fire is never quenched.
*~ **Mark 9:43-48***

We had had an unusual amount of rain one summer. Water seemed to get into cracks and crevices we never knew existed. Leaks seemed to appear out of nowhere, and with these leaks we sometimes found an even worse problem – black mold!

Sin is very much like black mold in our spiritual life. When we get lax in our faith, sin seems to find a way into our life, creating a very unhealthy spirit within us. We can try to "cover it up" or "wipe it away", but it will continue to return until we find the source of this sin in our lives and "cut it out". This does not necessarily mean that we need to cut off whatever part of our body is performing the sin, but find what is triggering the sin in the first place and omit it from our lives. Then, and only then, can we truly be cleansed in our spiritual life to be presentable to God.

What has been "seeping" into your life that is causing a "black mold" in your spiritual life? Find the source, get rid of it and ask God for forgiveness. He will place a new and right spirit within you to once again create a healthy spiritual life that is in communion with Him.

Prayer

Heavenly Father, we know we are not perfect, and yes, we even sometimes get lazy in our spiritual lives. Please help us to find whatever is displeasing to You in our lives and help us to rid ourselves of it so that we are once again presentable to You for use as you will have us do to further Your kingdom here on this earth. Amen.

TAKING SHELTER

You who live in the shelter of the Most High,
who abide in the shadow of the Almighty,*
will say to the Lord, 'My refuge and my fortress;
my God, in whom I trust.'
For he will deliver you from the snare of the fowler
and from the deadly pestilence;
he will cover you with his pinions,
and under his wings you will find refuge;
his faithfulness is a shield and buckler.
~ Psalm 91:1-4

Outside my window one morning, I noticed how nothing seemed to be stirring in the deep green of the ravine – no birds flitted about, no squirrels were seen amongst the foliage. The wind off of the lake spread the clouds over the sky, filtering any light that the sun tried to cast upon the ground. The hint of impending rain in the coolness of the morning breeze seemed heavy.

Then, after a few minutes, I noticed a heavily leaf-clothed branch bounce – a shimmer of movement, then another branch bounce. Movement soon gave way to a squirrel running along the branch, moving from limb to limb – tree to tree in the safety of the leafy covering. This squirrel was taking cover in the shelter of the trees while still getting about in his morning routine. If it were to start raining, he would still be in the shelter of the leaves of the tree. Yet, as the morning wore on, the clouds were pealed back, revealing another beautiful day ahead.

We, as Christians, can take shelter from the storms in our lives by keeping in close communion with God through prayer, Bible studies, worship. In this way, we can find the strength we need through turbulent times of our lives. When we go about our daily routines with God beside us, nothing and no one can harm or defeat us. This doesn't mean we won't feel the affects of the storm, but we will get through whatever life might rain down on us. God will deliver us to sunnier days ahead when we stand firm in our faith – taking shelter in His grace and love.

Prayer

Dearest Father in Heaven, thank you for sheltering us through the storms of this life and carrying us through to sunnier days ahead. May our faith remain strong as You cover us with Your love and grace. Amen.

REACHING UP AND CRYING OUT

O Lord, how many are my foes!
Many are rising against me;
many are saying to me,
'There is no help for you in God.'
Selah

But you, O Lord, are a shield around me,
my glory, and the one who lifts up my head.
I cry aloud to the Lord,
and he answers me from his holy hill.
Selah
*~ **Psalm 3:1-4***

There is a tree I see daily from my window that appears to be reaching up to the heavens with limbs stripped of foliage. It is as if it is crying out to God for help in its time of trial. Yet, if I really study the tree in more detail, it does still have some foliage here and there near the top, and even more nearer to the ground, where its roots are still holding fast to the ground – drawing its nourishment from the earth.

Like this tree, many of us have had times where we feel stripped of so much in our lives that we just cannot handle one more thing. We find ourselves reaching out to God and crying for help. Sometimes we feel that we are not being heard, because more things continue to pile upon us, even as we search for help from our Heavenly Father. He does not abandon us, though. He is always listening and He always answers us, although not always as quickly or in the ways we wish He would. If we really look more closely to our circumstances that we are crying out to Him about, we can begin to see a little bit of grace and support here and there that we may have at first overlooked. As we get closer to our faith in which we are rooted and grounded in, we may even find more sustenance that He is providing us, although we may not have realized it at first, such as in the love, support and prayers of people around us that He has provided as our faith family. He continues to give us what we need to continue living and growing, even in the most difficult circumstances.

What has you feeling like you need to cry out to God? What do you see around you as you look closer at what He has already provided for you? Who has He placed in your life to journey through this earthly life as your family – both blood-related and faith family? He has surrounded you with everything you need live this life of yours as long as you allow yourself to reach up and cry out for the help you need. He will not leave you to handle your trouble alone, because, as any loving parent does, He will take your hand and guide you when you really need it most - shielding you from the harm this world tries to bring down upon you.

Prayer

Lord, we know You hear our cries for help in our times of trouble. We know that You are always with us and have placed others here to help us through these times. We thank you for answered prayers and for Your love and protection as we persevere through this life we now live as we continue to look to You, our strength and our shield. Amen.

Do Not Fear

For I, the Lord your God,
hold your right hand;
it is I who say to you, 'Do not fear,
I will help you.'
*~ **Isaiah 41:13***

One winter, just before the first heavy snowfall, I watched a squirrel frantically digging below the bird feeder as he searched for any little tidbits he could for his meal. Having some old bread that needed to be tossed, I went to the door, unlocked and opened it to see a second squirrel standing on his hind legs, facing me with his front paws together, as if caught in a prayer for food. The first squirrel immediately ran to the nearest tree as I slowly opened the door, but the one that looked like he had been praying just watched me as I tossed the bread out for them to eat. He immediately went and began to eat his fill, while the other squirrel continued to watch from a distance.

People are always searching for fulfillment in their lives. Many fear the changes that come with turning their lives to Christ, so they run and hide – never finding the fulfillment that is right before their eyes. Those that prayerfully seek God's guidance in their lives find the fulfillment they have been searching for.

Like the squirrel that watched from afar as the one that waited to be fed enjoyed his meal, people that continue to hide from God can see the blessings bestowed on those that willingly give their lives to God. Eventually, even some that initially run and hide will come slowly and cautiously to also find the fulfillment in their lives that God offers once they see that He means them no harm and only wants the best for them as well.

Prayer

Heavenly Father, help those that are lost find You by seeing You reflected in me. May they see that a life with You is so much more fulfilling than trying to find fulfillment on their own. Amen.

GOD'S WATERED GARDEN

if you offer your food to the hungry
and satisfy the needs of the afflicted,
then your light shall rise in the darkness
and your gloom be like the noonday.
The Lord will guide you continually,
and satisfy your needs in parched places,
and make your bones strong;
and you shall be like a watered garden,
like a spring of water,
whose waters never fail.
*~ **Isaiah 58:10-11***

The ravine outside the window had been relatively dry and barren during the winter months, aside from a brief melting period after a heavy snow. It was then, when the stream came back to life that I began to really see the bustle of creatures in and around the trees along the flowing stream. Squirrels that I hadn't seen in months came out in groups to run around in search of food. Birds began to flit around the branches of what had been, just days before, silent branches tossed about in the winter winds.

Our spiritual lives can often feel barren when idleness sets in. When we do not go about doing the work God has placed us here to do, we are just dormant bodies inhabiting the earth. We are much like the dry streambed – useless in caring for the lives around us.

Yet, when we set about the task of sharing our blessings from God with others, we begin to see new growth in the lives around us. Just like supplying the stream with the water it needs to nourish the life growing around it, God will supply us with all that we need to care for others. We need not worry about running out of what we need to survive when we serve God, for He provides us with a "spring of water, whose waters never fail." As we water the souls of those in need, they will see God's light shining through us to help their spirits grow in God's garden of grace.

Prayer

Lord, fill me with Your loving spirit. Thank You for all you provide me with to serve others in Your name. Help me to use all You supply me with to the best of my ability to grow Your garden of believers with Your grace. Amen.

Behold the Beauty After the Storm

One thing I asked of the Lord,
that will I seek after:
to live in the house of the Lord
all the days of my life,
to behold the beauty of the Lord,
and to inquire in his temple.
~ Psalm 27:4

Worries surround us throughout our lives. Sometimes more so than others. They can sometimes affect us just slightly, like the light, powdery snows of winter that slow us down in our commutes or other times, they can weigh on us heavily, like the deep, wet snow storms that can keep up from going about our daily routines. Regardless, these worries have one thing in common – they keep our focus on ourselves and what we can do to resolve them as opposed to the One that wants only the best for us.

Beginning each day asking God to continue to help you through whatever might come your way throughout the day helps to remove the focus on yourself and put the worries of the day in God's hands. Knowing He will provide helps ease the burden of trying to "go it alone" - "…but for God all things are possible." (Matthew 19:26b). It is by putting these burdens in the hands of God that we can finally lift our eyes to see the beauty of the day – even in difficult times. Like the morning sun shining on the newly fallen snow from the storm from the previous evening that illumines the little "diamonds" within the drifts of snow, we can begin to see the good in the midst of difficulties we experience.

As we continue our conversations with God, we can ask for Him to reveal His blessings to us in all situations, knowing that He is with us always. It is by moving the focus away from ourselves and onto God that we can continue to seek out what He would have us do to continue a deeper relationship with Him. God has told us in Hebrews 13:5b, "I will never leave you or forsake you." Let us remember this even at the most difficult times in our lives, for there is beauty after the storm.

Prayer

Heavenly Father, our lives are not easy. Temptations and trials plaque us daily – sometimes more so than others. Help us to remember to always hand our worries over to You and allow You to move the focus of our lives away from ourselves and onto You and what You have in store for us after these storms are over. Amen.

Good Enough?

But now thus says the Lord,
he who created you, O Jacob,
he who formed you, O Israel:
Do not fear, for I have redeemed you;
I have called you by name, you are mine.
When you pass through the waters, I will be with you;
and through the rivers, they shall not overwhelm you;
when you walk through fire you shall not be burned,
and the flame shall not consume you.
~ Isaiah 43:1-2

Many people wonder if they are good enough. Good enough to have what they have, to have the family and friends that they are blessed with and yes, even to have the love of God. It may be that guilt of things they have done in the past still haunt them. They may feel that they are unforgivable because they cannot even forgive themselves.

God, however, loves us with a love that we cannot even fathom. How many of us would allow our own son or daughter to die a horrific death so that others can live? It is a question that leaves us wondering how far we would be willing to go to extend love beyond our wildest imaginations. Yet God did just that and more by allowing His Son to conquer death so that we could live and be reconciled to Him.

As our pastor often reminds us, "God loves you and there is nothing you can do about it." He is with us at all times – good and bad – walking beside us, waiting for us to lean on Him in times of trouble and to rejoice with Him during our celebrations. There is absolutely NOTHING we can do that will separate us from His love for us! We are His children, loved beyond any measure that we can explain. This make us "good enough" no matter how we may feel we measure up to what God has given us.

Prayer

Heavenly Father, it is unfathomable to us how much You love us, yet You remain steadfastly beside us, waiting for us to turn to you in our times of joy as well as sorrow. Thank You for being such a loving Father to us, despite our straying from time to time. Thank You for always calling us back to You and loving us beyond measure, Amen.

TAKE A MOMENT AND LIFT UP YOUR PRAISE

How lovely is your dwelling place,
O Lord of hosts!
My soul longs, indeed it faints
for the courts of the Lord;
my heart and my flesh sing for joy
to the living God.

Even the sparrow finds a home,
and the swallow a nest for herself,
where she may lay her young,
at your altars, O Lord of hosts,
my King and my God.
Happy are those who live in your house,
ever singing your praise.
Selah
~ Psalm 84:1-4

One morning, as I started to wind my way up to the church to begin my day of work, I spied a deer just to the left of the lane. I immediately stopped and grabbed my phone to take a picture of this lovely creature of God. I had been in a state of rushing and ignoring the beauty around me. I was not appreciating all that God continues to provide for me each and every day. This is something I am guilty of very frequently. I then drove the rest of the way up the lane to start my day of work having appreciated stopping to enjoy a glimpse of God's beautiful creation and moment to reflect on all He has blessed me with.

We often go about our day rushing to accomplish our agendas for the day. Our schedules are so full, that we don't always make the time to just be still and talk to our Creator. We don't take time to appreciate what He has given us and continue to look for more on our own without using what we already have. We have become captives in a vicious circle of wants and schedules that were not intended to be part of why we are here to begin with.

God created us to be loved by Him – to have a relationship with Him. He gave us all that we have and allows us to be stewards of these gifts meant to provide for our needs, not our wants. We are meant to share the surplus of these gifts with those that may need assistance – not hoard it for ourselves. Instead, we have allowed these gifts to become something that they were not meant to be – a vehicle that keeps us too busy to spend time where we need to most – in relationship with God.

Today, try to step back – find a quiet moment to reflect on the many blessings you have been given. Slow down and smell the flowers, listen to your loved ones around you, enjoy a moment with someone who needs your time. Then, lift your praises to the God of all creation, giving Him thanks for all He has given you and for the wisdom to carry out His will here on this earth.

Prayer

Father God, thank you for those moments that make us stop and reflect on all of the wonderful gifts you have given us. Thank you for entrusting us with these gifts. Help us to use them as You intended for us to, instead of for our own selfish ambitions. May we remember to slow down in our otherwise busy lives and take more time to praise Your mighty acts in our lives and be in relationship with You as Your children. Amen.

Continuing Education

Come, O children, listen to me;
I will teach you the fear of the Lord.
Which of you desires life,
and covets many days to enjoy good?
Keep your tongue from evil,
and your lips from speaking deceit.
Depart from evil, and do good;
seek peace, and pursue it.
*~ **Psalm 34:11-14***

Once summer has ended, we once again begin to see the yellow school buses transporting children – some excitedly and some reluctantly – returning to school. The school supplies carefully packed into new backpacks and carried by these students who are now equipped to learn new things throughout the coming school year. Some also carry lunches along with their school supplies to renew their strength during the day.

We as Christians also have our "school supplies" to refer to throughout this same school year. Our Bibles, devotionals, Bible study topic books and prayer journals are available to renew our spiritual strength as we feast upon God's Word, searching for more knowledge that will draw us closer in relationship to our Heavenly Father. Through this learning process, we are able to carry away precious bits of information that help us re-mold our way of thinking and communicate with others in more positive ways. This time of continuing education also helps us to better equip ourselves to walk in the light of Christ and away from the dark places that tend to tempt us away from our relationship with God. We can find inner peace by drawing nearer to the life God has us here to live out instead of a life that causes us guilt and distress as we inwardly recognize that we shouldn't be doing what we are doing.

It is back to school time. Pull out and dust off those Bibles and study materials that may have been neglected over the summer months and dive into God's Word. You may be surprised at all you will come to learn in the coming year.

Prayer

Lord God, help us to open our minds and hearts to learn what You would have us learn from You throughout the coming year. Make us find the time to set aside to delve into Your Word and savor the knowledge that it holds within is pages to help guide us through this life you have blessed us with. Amen.

WE ARE ONE

I therefore, the prisoner in the Lord,
beg you to lead a life worthy of the calling
to which you have been called,
with all humility and gentleness, with patience,
bearing with one another in love,
making every effort to maintain the unity of the Spirit
in the bond of peace.
There is one body and one Spirit,
just as you were called to the one hope of your calling,
one Lord, one faith, one baptism, one God and Father of all,
who is above all and through all and in all.
*~ **Ephesians 4:1-6***

A heavy snow is made up of so many snowflakes that we cannot count them. The overall effect can be a beautiful winter scene to look out upon once the snow has finished falling. The soft, white piles can then be blown into new shapes and formations as the wind so determines, creating an ever-changing landscape of a different loveliness than the first. Change happens, and with it, adaptations are made to enjoy the scenery of life as it is presents itself to us.

So, to are the changes and adaptations in our lives as we live with those around us. Not everyone is like us, just as no two snowflakes are the same. Alone, we are a beautiful original image of God, but together, we make and even more wonderful and engaging tapestry of God's ultimate design. We must learn to live together – with our many similarities, yet also with our differences, to create God's kingdom here on earth. We may all believe in God the Father, His Son - our Savior Jesus Christ, and His Holy Spirit, but yet we may also live our lives differently than that of the person next to us. Our entire being may not entirely agree with everything everyone else does or believes outside of just our belief of the Holy Trinity. This does not mean, however, that we cannot live and work and be as one in the body of Christ.

We all have someone within our family or friendships with whom we do not always agree, but do we love them any less for that? Do we disown them and ignore them or do we still try to overlook the differences between them and us and continue to associate with them? Our relationships are worth more than a disagreement over certain issues.

God loves each and every one of us, despite our short comings, our differences between each other and the many ways in which we may worship Him. God is the creator of us all and loves us all equally, and there is nothing we can do about it. We should also love one another the same way, despite our many differences. We can we still come together to worship God as one, just as the many snowflakes come together to create a beautiful winter landscape. We just have to agree to disagree with whatever someone else's views may be and accept and love them as our brothers and sisters in Christ, just as God also accepts all of us.

Prayer

Heavenly Father, help us to overcome our differences of opinion and realize that what is more important in this life is that we are one in You, that You love us all, despite our differences and that together, we can make a beautiful family of Your making here on earth as brothers and sisters together through Jesus Christ, Your Son. Amen.

PAIN OR PARADISE

He replied, 'Truly I tell you,
today you will be with me in Paradise.'
*~ **Luke 23:43***

Our church family had had a very rough few weeks. Many had suffered the loss of a family member or friend. I counted nine funeral notifications in two weeks. During the season of Lent, when we often reflect on our lives and setting ourselves right with God, we also remember all that Christ went through as He approached His ultimate reason for coming to us here on earth.

Christ told not only His disciples that they would see Him again, but even the thief hanging beside Him on the cross that "today you will be with me in Paradise." This is a promise that life does not end here on earth. Life continues on in a better place – one that we strive to achieve entrance to by doing as Christ has told us, *"Do not let your hearts be troubled. Believe in God, believe also in me."* (**John 14:1**) Christ also prayed to God, *"Father, I desire that those also, whom you have given me, may be with me where I am, to see my glory, which you have given me because you loved me before the foundation of the world."* (**John 17:24**)

Yes, we are allowed to mourn. Even Jesus mourned. Yet even after the time of mourning, there was time for celebration, for Lazarus was rescued from the grave. Those we have lost may not live here with us anymore, but they are living in a much better place – with Christ in Paradise. After our time of mourning, we may also celebrate that our lost loved ones have achieved their final victory over death. They have joined

Christ at His table with our Heavenly Father, where they will celebrate with Him for all eternity. We will see them once again when it is our turn to cross over from this life to our eternal life with Christ and join in this celebration as well.

Prayer

Lord, difficult times of loss bring us to our knees. We feel an emptiness that longs to be filled. Please fill us with Your love and Your peace - knowing that our lost loved ones are with You and that one day, you will have us join You for all eternity in Paradise, where we will all be reunited once again. Amen.

TAKE NOTICE

The voice of the LORD is over the waters;
the God of glory thunders,
the LORD, over mighty waters.
The voice of the LORD is powerful;
the voice of the LORD is full of majesty.
*~ **Psalm 29:3-4***

Thunder shakes the ground as the sheets of rain drive across the lawns and roadways. The darkness is strange for mid-morning, yet everyone is still going about their daily routines – some getting much wetter than others. Summer storms in the midst of extreme heat waves and humidity can be quite violent, yet when respected, we are able to stay safe amidst the driving storms while appreciating the life-giving waters that are coming down to sustain all creation. We can even marvel at the power within the storms themselves.

God shows His power in so many ways. Sometimes we see His power in strong ways, such as storms or during our times of trial. Other times we see it in the still, quiet moments of our lives when we glory in His creation all around us, or even in the smile of a small child.

Take notice of all God has done and is doing all around us. He is in control of everything. When we respect His divine plan and appreciate all that He continually gives us, we can be fully amazed and enjoy the gifts of His great majesty in our lives, no matter what form these gifts may take.

Prayer

Thank you, Heavenly Father, for the many gifts you give us each and every day. The life-giving rains, the strength we need during life's many trials, and even the power of a child's smile to warm our hearts with love help sustain us when we take notice of these very gifts you bless us with. Please help us to always remember that Your power and majesty that are always with us, for without You to remind us to do so, we easily forget this very fact when we go about our daily routines. Amen.

Then he returned from the region of Tyre,
and went by way of Sidon towards the Sea of Galilee,
in the region of the Decapolis. They brought to him a
deaf man who had an impediment in his speech;
and they begged him to lay his hand on him.
He took him aside in private, away from the crowd,
and put his fingers into his ears,
and he spat and touched his tongue.
Then looking up to heaven, he sighed and said to him, '
Ephphatha', that is, 'Be opened.'
And immediately his ears were opened,
his tongue was released, and he spoke plainly.
Then Jesus ordered them to tell no one;
but the more he ordered them,
the more zealously they proclaimed it.
They were astounded beyond measure, saying,
'He has done everything well;
he even makes the deaf to hear and the mute to speak.'
*~ **Mark 6:31-37***

At a women's mission study weekend, I was enlightened on how to better delve into some of the stories of the Gospel of Mark. When I turned each character of a story into me and tried to decide what I would have heard, felt, and seen during each story from the other characters, I was better able to understand each character in the story. This also helped me gain a whole new understanding of the stories contained in Mark. In this particular story, I saw the people of Decapolis, the deaf man with the speech impediment and Jesus.

Being one of the people of Decapolis, I would have no doubt heard the stories of Jesus working healings and performing miracles. Here was my chance to see if this man was the real deal. I wanted to see a miracle first-hand, so I found this man that was deaf and could not speak well. I was disappointed that Jesus did not perform the healing in front of me, though. Once the deaf man with the speech impediment was healed, however, I was so amazed that I had to share the story with everyone I knew that had not been there!

If I were Jesus, I had pity on the man yet I did not want to perform such a miracle in the midst of the crowd. I knew that they were thinking that I was a side show miracle worker and wanted to witness such a miracle healing before their very eyes. Taking the man aside privately to heal him was a way I had hoped to keep the talk down and still provide for this man the ability to hear and speak. I knew what my upcoming fate was going to be and that my enemies were trying to find a reason to kill me, but I still had much work to do before my crucifixion. I still looked to God for the power to carry out this healing, for all power given to me came from my Father in heaven. Once performed, I ordered everyone to keep this healing quiet, but they just would not listen to me. The more I said not to say anything, they more they talked to others about it.

As the deaf man with the speech impediment, I was overjoyed at being able to speak clearly and hear all that was going on around me. How could I possibly keep this story to myself? I had to tell the story of how I was deaf and unable to speak well, but now, because of this man Jesus, I was able to be free of those disabilities and communicate as everyone else around me did!

By looking at the stories in Mark in this manner, I was better able to come away with a sense of the joy that these people just could not contain, no matter how much Jesus communicated to them to stay quiet about it. How could I witness such a miracle and not share it with everyone I saw? Even today, I must share these stories with others to tell of the Good News of Jesus and all that he did and still does today in my life.

Prayer

Dearest Lord Jesus, I know that You had once wanted the many stories of Your miracles kept quiet so that You would have the time needed to carry out Your purpose on this earth. That time has come and gone. Now I am to share the Good News of all You have done for everyone throughout the world. Give me the power, the knowledge and the opportunities You want me to do this in and make me boldly proclaim You as my Lord and Savior so that others are able to proclaim the same. Amen.

Keeping the Sabbath

One sabbath he was going through the cornfields;
and as they made their way
his disciples began to pluck heads of grain.
The Pharisees said to him,
'Look, why are they doing what is not lawful
on the sabbath?' And he said to them,
'Have you never read what David did
when he and his companions were hungry
and in need of food? He entered the house of God,
when Abiathar was high priest,
and ate the bread of the Presence,
which it is not lawful for any but the priests to eat,
and he gave some to his companions.'
Then he said to them,
'The sabbath was made for humankind,
and not humankind for the sabbath;
so the Son of Man is lord even of the sabbath.'
*~ **Mark 2:23-28***

Jesus had a difficult ministry with the scurtiniy of the Pharisees upon him at all times. The Pharisees looked for even the smallest violation of the Ten Commandments to destroy the image of Jesus in the eyes of the people. They greatly disliked Jesus and the popularity he was gaining, for Jesus was turning their world upside down - challenging their authority at every turn. How could this man Jesus say such things? He had no authority to do so! At least that it what they LIKED to think!

Moses was given the Ten Commandments hundreds of years earlier, but they had since then been expanded upon and reinterpreted by the religious leaders. These reinterpretations created restrictions that were almost impossible to follow at all times. This especially was the case with the commandment of keeping the sabbath holy. If we look in **Deuteronomy 5:12-15**, it says, *"Observe the sabbath day and keep it holy, as the Lord your God commanded you. For six days you shall labour and do all your work. But the seventh day is a sabbath to the Lord your God; you shall not do any work—you, or your son or your daughter, or your male or female slave, or your ox or your donkey, or any of your livestock, or the resident alien in your towns, so that your male and female slave may rest as well as you. Remember that you were a slave in the land of Egypt, and the Lord your God brought you out from there with a mighty hand and an outstretched arm; therefore the Lord your God commanded you to keep the sabbath day."* To say that they could not do anything that looked like work made it difficult for individuals to even feed themselves!

God did not intend for the sabbath to be something to make life difficult for us - just another rule to break if not followed. This was a commandment for us to take a break from all of the work that we do in a normal week and take one day a week to just enjoy ourselves. We are to be able to rejuvenate ourselves by worshipping God, taking time out for our relationships and doing activities we might not always have time for during the rest of the week, or even just relaxing. With some occupations, the "sabbath" might not even fall on Sunday (or Saturday for the Jewish people).

There are people that tend to do whatever it takes to make more money. Sometimes this is working seven days a week for weeks on end with no break. THIS would be a violation of the commandment of the sabbath, for these individuals are not taking time for themselves to focus on God, work on their relationships and rest. They are putting themselves in a position to "burn out", work themselves into the grave or just mentally exhaust themselves to the point that even their relationships are neglected.

Be sure to keep the sabbath in your own life. Take time out for God, for your family and for yourself. Keep your relationships with God and family healthy and happy by giving them the attention they need, as well as keeping yourself grounded in Christ. In this way, the sabbath God commanded you to keep will make your life a much happier one.

Prayer

Lord, when the busy-ness of life keeps me running, help me to stop and remember to keep the sabbath to renew my relationship with you, with my family and just give me the rest and peace of mind I need to tackle another work week. Amen.

TAKING IT TO THE STREETS

Jesus went out again beside the lake;
the whole crowd gathered around him, and he taught them.
As he was walking along,
he saw Levi son of Alphaeus sitting at the tax booth,
and he said to him, '
Follow me.' And he got up and followed him.

And as he sat at dinner in Levi's house,
many tax-collectors and sinners
were also sitting with Jesus and his disciples
—for there were many who followed him.
When the scribes of the Pharisees
saw that he was eating with sinners and tax-collectors,
they said to his disciples, '
Why does he eat with tax-collectors and sinners?'
When Jesus heard this, he said to them,
'Those who are well have no need of a physician,
but those who are sick;
I have come to call not the righteous but sinners.'
*~ **Mark 2:13-17***

Jesus taught by example. He came to show us the way that God wanted us to live, not the way in which we had been living. We tend to stay where we are comfortable - in circles of friends and associates with the same values that we have. We do not like conflict or feeling out of place.

Christians today are still this way. Yes, there are those few that go out into the mission field and preach the Gospel to those who do not know Christ, but in relation to the number of people that claim they are christians, those in the mission field are a small percentage of the body of Christ. Going to church on Sunday often makes christians feel that they have done their duty for the week, but if they look at the example Christ set, they haven't quite hit the mark. They should be taking the message they have learned at church out to those who do not even know about Christ.

We must find ways to take the Good News of Christ out to the least, the lost and the lonely and share it with them. We must leave our "comfort zones" and walk where Christ would walk and talk with those Christ would want talk to. He didn't come to save those already following God. He came to save those that were not following God and lost in their sinful ways.

Where do you feel God calling you to share His Good News? What can you do to move from your comfort zone to take the message of Christ to the streets? Who will you help save for God's eternal kingdom? If we do not answer and act on these very questions, the world, as a whole, will never know the saving grace of Jesus Christ.

Prayer

Heavenly Father, move within me to feel Your calling to share the news of Christ with those that do not yet know Him. Help me to move out of my comfort zone and to the streets where You would have me be a christian in action in the name of Jesus. Help me to find Your lost sheep and bring them to Your eternal fold. Amen

CALL AND BE SAVED

But what does it say? 'The word is near you,
on your lips and in your heart'
(that is, the word of faith that we proclaim);
because if you confess with your lips that Jesus is Lord
and believe in your heart
that God raised him from the dead, you will be saved.
For one believes with the heart and so is justified,
and one confesses with the mouth and so is saved.
The scripture says,
'No one who believes in him will be put to shame.'
For there is no distinction between Jew and Greek;
the same Lord is Lord of all
and is generous to all who call on him.
For, 'Everyone who calls on the name of the Lord
shall be saved.'
*~ **Romans 10:8-13***

Sometimes I feel that I cannot possibly be worthy of the gift of eternal life. What makes me so special? I am obviously not perfect, no matter how hard I might try to be. I often stumble in this human life of mine. I may seem one way in public and another at home, where I am more comfortable to let my guard down. How can I possibly measure up to receive such a gift?

Paul said that if we confess with our lips and that Jesus is Lord and believe in our hearts that God raised him from the dead we will be saved. Our belief justifies us and our confession with our mouth saves us. It doesn't matter who we are, what we have done or where we live - God is the God of all of creation and will give this gift to all who call on the name of the Lord, who will save us from death.

What are you waiting for? Do you believe in Christ as your Lord and Savior? Have you confessed with your mouth and believed in your heart that Christ died and was raised to save you? If not, it is never too late to call and be saved!

Prayer

Dear God, I thank you for the gift of Your one and only Son, who You gave to save me from sin and death. I believe Jesus died and rose again to reconcile me to You. Please, take what life I have left and use me as you will to further Your kingdom by bringing others to this same knowledge that You have revealed to me. In the name of Christ, my Lord. Amen.

Applying Your "Oxygen Mask"

then the Lord God formed man from the dust of the ground,
and breathed into his nostrils the breath of life;
and the man became a living being.
*~ **Genesis 2:7***

Preflight instructions by the stewardesses always include what to do when the oxygen masks drop down from the ceiling. You are to "put on your own mask before assisting others." Without enough oxygen flowing to your brain, you won't be much help to others. You may "pass out" before helping all those others that are unable to put their own masks on.

The same is with our spiritual life. Unless we breathe in the Word of God and fill ourselves with His life-giving message of love, life and hope, we won't be able to help others very far in their spiritual journey. We will "burn out" before helping those that need help finding God at work in their lives.

Today, make it a point to "put on your oxygen mask" of God's message to you through His Word, prayer and time meditating on all the wonderful works He is doing in your life. Then help others find their "oxygen masks" of faith as well. You will be much more effective helping others when you first care for your own spiritual wellness.

Prayer

Dear Lord, breathe in me Your breath of life so that I can be a useful instrument to lead others to Your life-saving love. Amen.

From Darkness to Light

For it is the God who said, 'Let light shine out of darkness',
who has shone in our hearts
to give the light of the knowledge of the glory of God
in the face of Jesus Christ.
~ 2 Corinthians 4:6

December had been more cloudy than light outside. The gray, dreary days tended to put one into a somber mood, even with the knowledge of Christmas approaching. This darkness could really put a damper on the festivities when rain and/or snow caused the body to ache with stiffness and soreness in the joints.

This dreary darkness reminds me of the world into which our Savior was born. It was groaning under the weight of sin that had accumulated over the centuries after that first sin of disobedience by Adam and Eve. The darkness needed to be overcome and it is with this beautiful gift from our Heavenly Father that the Light of Hope was born in a lowly stable so many years ago. It is with this gift of Light that we are drawn to that brings us out of the darkness of our own sin and eventual death to a new eternal life with Christ.

What a wonderful gift from our Father who created us! May we strive to live in the Light He has provided for us to lead us back to Him. May we also share this Light with others, so that they, too, may find their way back from the darkness.

Prayer

Dearest Lord Jesus, thank You for being our Light of Hope leading us out of the darkness to an eternal life with You. Amen.

From Mourning to Thanksgiving

You have turned my mourning into dancing;
you have taken off my sackcloth
and clothed me with joy,
so that my soul may praise you and not be silent.
O Lord my God, I will give thanks to you for ever.
~ Psalm 30:11-12

When we lose a loved one, we feel a void, a sense of walking in a fog with reality being something that has totally left us. We may cry out, "Where is God? I do not feel Him here beside me! I cannot hear Him speaking to me to tell me what to do."

God never leaves us. Sometimes we do not feel His presence when a pain so deep invades our life. We must mentally try to remember that He is still with us - carrying us through the difficulties of life. We might even experience His presence differently than we are used to - be it in the kind words offered to us by friends and family, feeling His presence with us with every embrace of those around us, and even in those helping us with all of the tasks we just cannot bear to do alone.

It is in these darkest moments of life that we can look to those that God has placed around us to help us regain our stability after such a heavy blow. The help that God provides allows us to be able to praise Him and give Him thanks. Yes, the pain is still there, but we are never alone. Even when those God has placed in our lives to help us go home, God is still holding us at all times - even in the quiet of the night - protecting us and giving us the strength and peace we need to carry on. God will even one day help us to find joy again, because He is always with us.

Prayer

Father in Heaven, thank You for always being with us and never leaving us. Even when we may experience times of deep loss that dull our senses, You are still there to see us through whatever comes our way. Help us to always remember that You show Your presence around us in many ways and to thank You and praise You. You will help us to experience joy in our lives again. Amen.

EXULT IN THE LORD!

But let all who take refuge in you rejoice;
let them ever sing for joy.
Spread your protection over them,
so that those who love your name may exult in you.
~ Psalm 5:11

We have all gone through times of trial. It may have been a grave illness, loss of job or a loved one, something that had started out as a joyous celebration and suddenly ended as a great disappointment, even the chaos of tumultuous storms or earth-shattering events. No matter what the trial might have been, these trials in life are never easy while going through them.

When events and circumstances try to lay us at the feet of despair, we must remember to hold fast to the One that is always beside us – loving us through it all. God will protect us from whatever trouble comes our way. We only need to give the weight of the trials of life over to God and continue to praise Him, no matter what we experience.

Like Job, who went through many losses in his life – his health, his wealth and his children – he continued to remain faithful to God. Job refused to blame God for his suffering. God rewarded Job's faithfulness with much more than he had lost before his suffering.

Always exult in the Lord, for He is the all-powerful constant in our lives that we can hold on to. He loves us and there is nothing we can do to change that fact. We must sing our praises long and loud of our loving Heavenly Father! He will reward us for our faithfulness to Him – if not in this life, definitely in the eternal life to come.

Prayer

Dear Lord, help us to always remember that You are with us through all that we go through in life. Help us to hold fast to You – remaining faithful and exulting in You at all times. Amen.

Glory in the Midst of Illness

Now a certain man was ill, Lazarus of Bethany,
the village of Mary and her sister Martha.
Mary was the one who anointed the Lord with perfume
and wiped his feet with her hair;
her brother Lazarus was ill.
So the sisters sent a message to Jesus,
'Lord, he whom you love is ill.'
But when Jesus heard it, he said,'
This illness does not lead to death;
rather it is for God's glory,
so that the Son of God may be glorified through it.'
~ John 11:1-4

A gentle breeze blew the branches of the trees beside the ravine, gently raising and lowering the branches, as if I was watching a chest rise and fall with each breath the tree was taking. With each breath, a few fall leaves would gently float to the ground in a small pile of gold. Suddenly, a stronger gust would more violently shake the tree, as if it was having a coughing fit, shaking an even greater number of leaves into the air to gently fall in a shower of gold. The trees were slowly coming into the end of their season of showing life for me to enjoy in my leisure.

Illness comes upon most people at some point in life. Some are minor illnesses, yet others lead to the end of an earthly existence. Some illnesses involve the mind, organs or extremities, yet others involve the ability to even breathe efficiently without racking the entire body with fits of coughing.

Illness does not necessarily lead to eternal death, but rather just a transition from this life to eternal glory. Other times, illness shows the glory of God through miraculous healing or even just in the loving care of those He sends to care and nurse the sick.

Illness does not have to be looked upon as a total negative of life, although no one wants to ever have to be sick. It can also have a silver lining that must be looked for ever so carefully. Perhaps it will bring someone back into relationship with someone they had had a falling out with quite some time ago, or even back to a deeper relationship with God, whom they might not have bothered to think about until the illness hit.

Next time an illness hits, look for the glory of God working in and through it. It is always there – hidden somewhat from immediate recognition. It just needs to be found and then give God thanks for the opportunity to experience it, even though it is not necessarily the easier way one likes to find His glory around them.

Prayer

Heavenly Father, none of us ever wants to be ill, nor do we wish illness on others. We know that everything is done for Your Glory. Help us to always be able to find a way to glorify You through even the most serious illnesses of life. Amen.

Index by Page Number

Index by Title

Index by Biblical Reference

About the Author

Wendy Miller met her husband in the church choir in 1987 when he had just finished student teaching. They married a year and a half later. Together, they have two married children, one grandson and triplet granddaughters on the way as of the publishing of this devotional book. When she is not working, Wendy enjoys traveling with her husband, visits with her family, reading, watching TV, crocheting and knitting.

She has worked as the Business Manager of her church since 2004. Her title makes her the "jack of all trades - master of none." She oversees the day to day operation of the church, scheduling of events and activities, as well as handling the newsletter, e-mail and app announcements, membership records and accounts payable.

Wendy is a member of The United Methodist Women, serving at the local level as treasurer since 2008. She has also served for the Aurora District UMW as Treasurer from 2009 to 2012 and Secretary between 2013 and 2014. She then served as Treasurer for the Northern Illinois Conference UMW from 2015 through 2019.

She is the Treasurer for the Northern Illinois Conference PAUMCS (Professional Administrators of the United Methodist Connectional Structure), for which she has been a member since 2004. Wendy has been a member of the National PAUMCS since 2005 and currently serves on the Professional Training and Standards Committee for this organization.

Wendy earned her Certification as a United Methodist Professional Administrator in 2014 and her Advanced Certification in 2018. The Advanced Certification culminated in the completion of a group project with three other United Methodist Administrators across the country in producing a guide to funeral planning that will be used across the United Methodist denomination. This guide is currently on the paumcs.org web site under the resources tab. The hope is that this guide will also be on the UMCOM web site in the near future.

This book of devotions had been written intermittently between 2006 and 2019. It is the hope of the author that these devotions help to inspire those searching for a closer relationship with God and give hope to those going through difficult times. May God bless all who read these devotions.

Made in the USA
Monee, IL
30 September 2020